MONUMENTS OF ENDLESSE
LABOURS

Lyndwood's *Provinciale*, showing title-page of the 1506 edition.
This particular copy belonged to Michaelhouse, Cambridge.

By permission of Cambridge University Library.

Monuments of Endlesse Labours

ENGLISH CANONISTS
AND THEIR WORK,
1300–1900

J. H. BAKER

THE HAMBLEDON PRESS

WITH THE ECCLESIASTICAL LAW SOCIETY

LONDON AND RIO GRANDE

Published by The Hambledon Press 1998

102 Gloucester Avenue, London NW1 8HX (UK)
PO Box 162, Rio Grande, Ohio 45674 (USA)

The Ecclesiastical Law Society
c/o 1 The Sanctuary, Westminster, London SW1P 3JT

ISBN 1 85285 167 8

A description of this book is available from
the British Library and from the Library of Congress

Typeset by Carnegie Publishing Ltd, Chatsworth Rd, Lancaster
Printed on acid-free paper and bound in Great Britain by
Cambridge University Press

Contents

Illustrations

Preface

N SO FAR as they are still visible through the dust, those 'monuments of ... endlesse and invincible labours' bemoaned in his wearier moments by Henry Swinburne (see page 62) are books which many of us still consult in our work, whether we are canonistic scholars, church officials, legal practitioners, ecclesiastical historians or mere common lawyers like me. While a history of canonists is by no means an introduction to canon law, as a body of jurisprudence, it is perhaps a necessary introduction to some of the sources from which we learn about it. This is an attempt to set them, in a non-technical way, in some kind of context, including the rise and fall – and finally the virtual disappearance – of the tradition of learning which they represented. It is gratifying to note that the learning was never wholly extinguished, and that the Ecclesiastical Law Society will ensure its survival into the next millennium.

The essays here have been reprinted, with slight rearrangement and emendation, from a series entitled 'Famous English Canonists' which appeared in the *Ecclesiastical Law Journal* between 1988 and 1997. If anyone should wonder why a common lawyer ever presumed to write on canonists and their work, the explanation is simple enough. The late Chancellor Graham Routledge, who was the begetter of the Ecclesiastical Law Society and a former colleague at Cambridge, twisted my arm to do it when the society was inaugurated in Cambridge in 1987, dismissing my proffered excuses with the reasonable assertion that every legal historian ought to know at least something about the makers of ecclesiastical law. Having rashly agreed to begin the series, I felt obliged by my original undertaking to continue until the end, and was kept to the mark by the kindly encouragement of Chancellor Michael Goodman as editor of the *Journal*. More to be wondered at, perhaps, is the reprinting of the articles in such handsome form, at the behest of the society, since they can only be regarded as interim sketches until a proper history of the canon law in England is written – and I am happy to record that it *is* now being written, though not, of course, by me. Their re-emergence in a collected version has nevertheless given me the opportunity to revise them lightly, and to add some illustrations, though I have not tried to supply all the omissions which have occurred to me. If I have given short shrift to some figures, and some periods, I can only plead that the essays were written against deadlines, and that I do not wish to pretend that this is any more than a collection of essays.

J. H. B.

Acknowledgements

 OR permission to reproduce illustrations, the publishers are grateful to Cambridge University Library, the Treasurer and Masters of the Bench of the Inner Temple, the Very Rev. the Dean of York, and the author. Particular acknowledgments will be found with the caption to each illustration.

The author wishes to express his gratitude to Chancellor Michael Goodman and to Mr Martin Sheppard for their editorial help and valuable comments at both stages in the emergence of this collection.

Abbreviations

ote: books were published in London unless a place of publication is given. Law reports are cited by the abbreviations currently used by lawyers; those from before 1865 may be found in the *English Reports* reprint.

ad v.	*see* gl. ad v.
BL	British Library, London.
C.	Constitutio (referring to the provincial constitutions).
c.	chapter (of a statute).
CUL	Cambridge University Library.
Co. Litt.	Coke upon Littleton, i.e. E. Coke, *First Part of the Institutes* (1628).
DNB	*Dictionary of National Biography* (2nd impression, repaginated, 1921).
gl. ad v.	glossa ad verbum (*vel* verba).
PCC	Prerogative Court of Canterbury will registers (now in the Public Record Office, class PROB 11).
tit.	titulus (referring to the titles of the provincial constitutions).
YB	Year Books.

Table of Statutes

Table of Provincial Legislation

Table of Cases

I

The Beginnings of
an English Canon Law
Tradition

HE academic study of canon law as an intellectual discipline began in twelfth-century
Bologna. At the flourishing law school which
had sprung up following the rediscovery of Justinian's *Digest*, Gratian began in the second quarter of the
century to apply the juristic method to the decretals, in order
to harmonise the 'discordant canons' of the church, and his
Decretum soon became the basis of a new form of scholarship.[1] Within a generation the new wave of learning reached
England,[2] where scholars returning from Bologna or Paris
settled in Canterbury, Exeter, Lincoln, Worcester and other
cathedral towns. Such was the fervour of decretistic study
in the wake of Gratian that a modern writer has even been
moved to claim the late twelfth century as 'the period when

---

1 See S. Kuttner, 'The Revival of Jurisprudence' in *Renaissance and
Renewal in the 12th Century*, ed. R. L. Benson and G. Constable
(Cambridge, Massachusetts, 1982), pp. 299–323; reprinted in
Studies in the History of Medieval Canon Law (Aldershot, 1990),
ch. 3. For the development of civil law studies in England, cf.
P. Stein, introduction to *The Teaching of Roman Law in England
around 1200*, Selden Society, Supplementary Series, 8 (1990).
2 M. Cheney, 'The Compromise of Avranches of 1172 and the
Spread of Canon Law in England', *English Historical Review*, 56
(1941), pp. 177–97.

English canonists made their most original and distinctive contributions to the history of canon law'.3 By the 1190s a law school had been established at Oxford, and it rapidly became one of the principal attractions of the nascent university there.4 Some *quaestiones disputatae* and glosses from the late 1190s – mostly attributable to Masters John of Tynemouth, Simon of Sywell and Nicholas de l'Aigle – are preserved in manuscripts in the British Library and at Gonville and Caius College, Cambridge,5 and three of the disputations have been printed by Professor Brundage.6

The earliest English canonists were avid collectors of decretals, and it is not surprising that their study of casuistic texts was coupled with a desire to tease out distinctions through teaching and debate. Their expositions of the decretals, inspired by Gratian, included the important *Summa quaestionum* (*c.* 1190) by Master Honorius, Vicar-

3 C. Duggan, *Canon Law in Medieval England* (1982), ch. 1, p. 374. The classic study is S. Kuttner and E. Rathbone, 'Anglo-Norman Canonists of the Twelfth Century', *Traditio*, 7 (1949–51), pp. 279–358; reprinted with further notes ('Retractationes') in *Gratian and the Schools of Law* (1983), ch. 8.

4 See R. W. Southern in *History of the University of Oxford*, i, ed. J. I. Catto (Oxford, 1984), at pp. 15–21. The first two centuries of law teaching at Oxford are traced with deep learning by Fr L. E. Boyle, 'Canon Law before 1380', ibid., pp. 531–64.

5 BL, Royal MS 9 E. VII, fos 191r–199r (*quaestiones* with references to 'Jo. de Thi. ', Master Simon, and other masters); Gonville and Caius College, Cambridge, MS 676 (glosses referring to 'Jo. de Ti.'); Kuttner and Rathbone, 'Anglo-Norman Canonists', pp. 317–27. Sywell was a papal judge delegate in the 1190s and a Canon of Lincoln. Tynemouth was a papal judge delegate *c.* 1210, and Archdeacon of Oxford at the time of his death (*c.* 1221).

6 J. A. Brundage, 'A Twelfth-Century Oxford Disputation concerning the Privileges of the Knights Hospitallers', *Medieval Studies*, 24 (1962), pp. 153–60; 'The Crusade of Richard I: Two Canonical *Quaestiones*', *Speculum*, 38 (1963), pp. 443–52; 'The Treatment of Marriage in the *Quaestiones Londinenses*', *Manuscripta*, 19 (1975), pp. 86–97. See also J. Brundage, *Medieval Canon Law* (1995), pp. 220–21.

General of York, probably composed while he was in France; and the even earlier *Decreta minora*, written by Odo of Dover, of which only charred fragments remain in the Cottonian collection.[7] But their principal literary output was a series of works on procedure.[8] For the most part these seem not to be descriptive accounts of actual procedure, in England or anywhere else, so much as speculative works intended to be of universal application. Notable among them were the *Practica legum et decretorum* (*c.* 1183/89) of William Longchamp (Chancellor of England, † 1197),[9] the *Ordo judiciarius* (*c.* 1196) of 'Ricardus Anglicus' (probably Richard de Mores, Prior of Dunstable, † 1241), written at Bologna,[10] and the *Summa aurea* (1239) of William of Drogheda († 1245), an Irishman who taught both laws at Oxford.[11] Of this last, Maitland has given us a lively assessment:

> In a certain sense his book is academic: that is, it was meant in the first instance for the Oxford law school. On the other hand, it is intensely practical. He is going to teach his readers to win causes, and begs that a few of the fees that they earn may purchase masses for his soul. His object is to trace an action through all its stages, to

7 Kuttner and Rathbone, 'Anglo-Norman Canonists', pp. 293, 304–16; Brundage, *Medieval Canon Law*, p. 213 n. 14.

8 See L. Fowler-Magerl, *Ordo iudiciorum vel ordo iudiciarius*, Ius Commune, Sonderhefte, 19 (Frankfurt, 1984).

9 Ed. E. Caillemer, in *Mémoires de l'Académie Nationale de Caen* (Caen, 1883), pp. 204–26. See Kuttner and Rathbone, 'Anglo-Norman Canonists', p. 290.

10 For this identification (rejecting Richardson's suggestion of R. de Lacy), see Kuttner and Rathbone, 'Anglo-Norman Canonists', pp. 329–39; Brundage, *Medieval Canon Law*, pp. 223–24.

11 Both Anglicus and Drogheda have been printed, ed. L. Wahrmund (Innsbruck, 1914). For this genre, see F. W. Maitland, *Roman Canon Law in the Church of England* (Cambridge, 1898), ch. 3; H. G. Richardson, 'The Oxford Law School under John', *Law Quarterly Review*, 57 (1941), pp. 319–38; J. E. Sayers, *Papal Judges Delegate in the Province of Canterbury* (Oxford, 1971), pp. 42–54.

solve the questions about procedure which will beset the practitioner, to supply him with useful formulas or models for the various documents which he may have to indite, and to offer him sound advice in the shape of *cautelae* ...[12]

It is to be hoped that Drogheda's students reaped the rewards so confidently promised to them, because their master was to need the masses sooner than he might have predicted. His murder, only a few years later, prevented the full achievement of the treatise he had in mind; but the character of his Oxford course is clear enough. The concentration on procedure was not peculiar to the canonists, and Drogheda's practical method of guidance is closely matched by the law-French procedural literature which, at around the same time, was being generated by lectures for students of the common law.[13] A law teacher was less concerned to impart abstract principles of jurisprudence than to tell his listeners how to get cases into court, and how to win them when they got there.

It is thought that the fission of the Oxford law school into two faculties of civil and canon law occurred shortly after the promulgation of the Gregorian decretals in 1234, which added a large new body of texts to the lecture curriculum. The first known doctor of canon law (around 1235) was Richard de Wyche († 1253), who became Saint Richard of Chichester, while Drogheda is mentioned in the same decade as a doctor of civil law.[14] The same period saw the

---

12 Maitland, *Roman Canon Law in England*, p. 110.

13 *Brevia placitata*, ed. G. J. Turner, Selden Society, 66 (1947); *Casus placitorum*, ed. W. H. Dunham, Selden Society, 69 (1950); P. Brand, 'Courtroom and Schoolroom: The Education of Lawyers in England Prior to 1400', *Bulletin of the Institute of Historical Research*, 60 (1987), pp. 147–65.

14 Boyle, 'Canon Law before 1380', at pp. 534–36.

establishment of a faculty of canon law at Cambridge.[15] Indeed, the only lawyers mentioned in the earliest Cambridge University statutes (*c.* 1245/50) are decretistae, rather than civilians,[16] though a Cambridge doctor of civil law is mentioned in the 1250s.[17] The two branches of Romanistic jurisprudence were in practice interdependent, since one could not become a canonist without studying Roman civil law; yet it was the study of canon law which led to place and preferment, not only in the legal sphere as judges or counsel but also in administrative and diplomatic positions, and it was regarded as an ideal qualification for the episcopacy.[18]

Those who were active in the day to day work of the English ecclesiastical courts began during the thirteenth century to constitute a distinct legal profession,[19] and they generated the demand for a slender literature concerned with English practice.[20] By the end of the century the advocates

15 For the early days of the Cambridge faculty of canon law, see J. A. Brundage, 'The Cambridge Faculty of Canon Law and the Ecclesiastical Courts of Ely', in *Medieval Cambridge*, ed. P. Zutshi (Woodbridge, 1993), pp. 21–45. Cf. D. R. Leader, *A History of the University of Cambridge*, i (Cambridge, 1988), pp. 192–201 (mainly on the later medieval period).

16 M. B. Hackett, *The Original Statutes of Cambridge University* (Cambridge, 1970), pp. 130–31, 203, 207.

17 A. B. Emden, *Biographical Register of the University of Cambridge to 1500* (Cambridge, 1963), p. 17.

18 This remained true in the following two centuries. Boyle, 'Canon Law before 1380', at p. 553, points out that one third of Edward III's bishops were law graduates.

19 P. Brand, 'The Other Legal Profession', in *The Origins of the English Legal Profession* (Oxford, 1992), pp. 143–57.

20 For early tracts on Arches procedure, see C. Donahue, introduction to *Select Cases from the Ecclesiastical Courts of the Province of Canterbury, c. 1200–1301*, Selden Society, 95 (1981), p. xxiv; and 'Consuetudines et observancie non scripte apud archus London. in appellationibus tuitoriis' (fourteenth century), BL, Royal MS 6 E. VI, fo. 403v.

and proctors in the Court of Arches had become a regulated body of professional lawyers,[21] composed entirely of law graduates,[22] and selected from a wide field.[23] Discipline was imposed through the medium of compulsory oaths, which bound the advocates to work honestly and expeditiously – and, under a constitution of 1273, to refrain from taking contingent fees. Among the statutes made by Archbishop Winchelsey for the Arches in 1295 were some which attempted to regulate even the private life of the advocates and proctors, who were evidently tending to become too worldly: they were not to enter taverns, unless driven to do so by necessity (which cannot, warned the archbishop, be expected to happen often); they were not to keep concubines or wander around at night; and they were not to frequent public entertainments ('publica spectacula').[24]

We know the names of many of the practitioners and

21 For what is known of the thirteenth-century advocates and proctors, and their professional regulation, see C. Donahue, introduction to *Select Cases from the Ecclesiastical Courts of the Province of Canterbury*, pp. 22–25; Brand, *Origins of the English Legal Profession*, pp. 146–54.

22 A constitution of Archbishop Pecham (1281) required at least three years' study of civil and canon law, which Lyndwood later held insufficient for heavy cases (*causae graves*) and applicable only to practice in inferior courts: [C. Lambeth, tit. 26], 'Veloces', in *Provinciale* (Oxford, 1679), pp. 75–76, gl. ad v. *Per triennium*. Archbishop Winchelsey (1295) required at least four years' legal study ('per quinquennium, vel quadriennium ad minus'), and a year's attendance on the Court of Arches: Statutes for the Court of Arches (1295) in *Concilia Magnae Britanniae*, ed. D. Wilkins (1737), ii, p. 205. The later requirement of a doctorate was customary rather than legislative: below, pp. 58–59 n. 7.

23 Winchelsey (last note) introduced selection by imposing a quota (sixteen), a similar measure to that which produced a closed order of serjeants at law in the Common Bench at much the same time. York followed suit in 1311 with a quota of twelve. See Brand, *Origins of the English Legal Profession*, pp. 150–51.

24 *Concilia Magnae Britanniae*, ed. D. Wilkins (1737), ii, pp. 27 (1273), 206 (1295).

judges in the higher ecclesiastical courts, and of the 'doctors of decretals' lecturing in Oxford and Cambridge during this century; yet they are for the most part shadowy figures. It is only in the early fourteenth century that we begin to see English lawyers making a significant and permanent individual impact on both the practice and the literature of canon law.

2

William Paull

EFORE we come to the well-known names associated with Bishop Bateman, we should notice
a near contemporary of his who has recently
been rescued from the shadows by Fr Leonard
Boyle.[1] Dr William Paull, though learned in the law, chose
the humble life of a parish priest rather than the authority
of judicial or episcopal office; and, despite the distinction
of his writing, none of his larger works has ever been printed
in full. Nevertheless, such was his reputation in his own
time that he may now be claimed as a major English canonistic writer worthy to begin our catalogue.[2]

Sometimes known by his Latin name, Willelmus de Pagula, our author himself spelt his surname 'Poul'.[3] But we

---

1 There are other unpublished texts: e.g., the Oxford lectures of
William Catchpole (Cachepol) († 1369), which refer to the opinions of other English canonists, are to be found in BL, Royal
MS 9 E. VIII. For another near contemporary, see W. Ullmann,
'John Baconthorpe as a Canonist', in *Church and Government in
the Middle Ages*, ed. C. N. L. Brooke et al. (Cambridge, 1976),
pp. 223–46. Dr Baconthorpe († 1346) might best be characterised
as a canonistic theologian.

2 What follows is based on the papers by Fr Boyle, which are all
conveniently reprinted (with others) in L. E. Boyle, *Pastoral Care,
Clerical Education and Canon Law, 1200–1400* (1981). The reprint
retains the pagination of the original articles.

3 L. E. Boyle, 'The *Summa summarum* and Some Other English
Works of Canon Law', *Proceedings of the 2nd International Congress of Medieval Canon Law* (Vatican City, 1965), pp. 415–56,
at pp. 418–19 n. 20.

have modernised it as Paull,4 since it derives from the place
of that name in Yorkshire, which in turn derives from the
ferry (L. *pagula*) on the River Humber east of Hull.5 Dr
Paull was an Oxford man, and probably took his doctorate
in canon law around 1320. He was ordained priest in Canterbury Cathedral on 1 June 1314 as Vicar of Winkfield,6
and held that benefice (in Windsor Forest) until his death
in 1332, serving also as an official 'penitentiary' in Berkshire
(first for the deanery of Reading, and later for that of Berkshire); but he is not known for certain to have enjoyed any
other preferments.7 This was, perhaps, an unusual course
of life for a scholar,8 though it accounts for Paull's interest
in and experience of confessional practice and pastoral problems, and it helps to explain why his literary output seems
not to have grown out of a course of university teaching –
as did most canonistic writing – but rather from a desire to
provide parsons and other clerics with a series of manuals
for their everyday guidance. Although the blinding effect of
the printing press would later serve to remove him from the
eyes of scholars, in his day Paull's reputation was equalled

4 He must not be confused, however, with his near contemporary
   William de Paul († 1349), Bishop of Meath: J. G. Fotheringham,
   'William Pagula', in *DNB*, xv, p. 66. The confusion occurs in Bale,
   Leland and other early bibliographical writers: A. F. Pollard, 'William de Paul', in *DNB*, xv, p. 521. See also Emden, *Biographical
   Register of the University of Oxford*, iii, pp. 1436–37.
5 This was a different Humber ferry from the one so well known
   to common lawyers, which was at Hessle, to the west of Hull.
6 J. R. Wright, *The Church and the English Crown, 1305–1334*
   (Toronto, 1980), p. 199 n. 19.
7 In the *Summa summarum* he apparently refers to himself in one
   passage as a Canon of St Paul's, London: L. E. Boyle, 'The *Oculus
   sacerdotis* and Some Other Works of William of Pagula', *Transactions of the Royal Historical Society*, fifth series, 5 (1955),
   81–110, at p. 100 n. 4. But no confirmation of this has been found,
   and he is not listed in Le Neve's *Fasti*.
8 So says W. A. Pantin, *The English Church in the Fourteenth Century* (Cambridge, 1955), pp. 28, 196, 218, referring to Paull.

only by John Ayton.[9] Indeed, he and Ayton share the distinction of being the only two English canonist writers of the fourteenth century whose works are commonly found in medieval book-lists.[10]

His books, which will be briefly described in turn, seem all to have been written in the 1320s, soon after his creation as a doctor of law. The *Summa summarum* was written in the period 1319–22.[11] Fr Boyle says it is 'a compilation of canon law and theology of five books and almost 350,000 words designed to provide every cleric, from parish priest to prelate, with an authoritative answer to every possible question that might arise out of his state or obligations. It is the only manual of canon law from an English source that can compare with the *Copiosa* of Hostiensis or the *Speculum* and *Reportorium* of Durandus ...'[12] The book was not written specifically for lawyers; but it provided the reader, whether legally trained or not, with a compendium of canon law and pastoral theology which would answer their every question, supporting the answer with the relevant authorities. It did not purport to be an original work, but rather a distillation from the best of the previous *summae*. For this reason the work was put out anonymously, though a manuscript at Christ's College, Cambridge, attributes it to William 'de Pabula',[13] and Fr Boyle has discovered internal evidence to connect it with Paull's *Oculus*.[14] Its arrangement was based on the famous *Summa* of the Spanish canonist Raymund de Peñafort († 1275), and the five

9 For Ayton (or Acton), see below, p. 29.
10 Boyle, 'The *Summa summarum*', p. 416.
11 Ibid., pp. 415–56.
12 Boyle, 'The *Oculus sacerdotis*', p. 101.
13 Christ's College, Cambridge, MS 2, fo. 269r, quoted by Boyle, 'The *Summa summarum*', p. 420 n. 24.
14 Boyle, 'The *Summa summarum*', pp. 422, 433.

constituent books deal with the following topics: (i) sources of law and authority, including the role of judges; (ii) actions and legal procedure; (iii) the clergy; (iv) marriage; (v) criminal offences. The books are divided into 257 chapters,[15] more than three-quarters of them corresponding with headings in Raymund. Many of the additional chapters are based on the equally famous *Reportorium* (or *Répertoire*) of 'Durandus', the French canonist Guillaume Durand († 1296). Paull goes further than his sources, however, in suggesting answers to questions; he also incorporates English provincial legislation, English customs, and even the provisions of Magna Carta; and he works in a good deal of theology. The result is an encyclopaedic work of ready reference, and as such it achieved an original authority which its author did not claim. It circulated widely, and at least thirteen surviving manuscripts are known. It was much broader in scope than the work of Drogheda, Ayton or Lyndwood, and probably of more practical use. Fr Boyle has printed the prologue and the table of contents.[16]

Paull also wrote a book called the 'Priest's Eye' (*Oculus sacerdotis*).[17] This is in three parts, each named in the ophthalmic mode: the *Pars oculi* (written last, and dealing with confessional practice and what we should call penology), the *Dextera pars oculi* (dealing with pastoral questions and the teaching of practical morality) and the *Sinistra pars oculi* (a theological discourse on the seven sacraments). This was obviously intended for the guidance of parish priests, and combined theological and legal information with homely hints – for example, about looking after children. Professor Davis thought the book diffuse, repetitive and

15 See the table printed ibid., pp. 443–51.
16 Ibid., pp. 440–43.
17 Boyle, 'The *Oculus sacerdotis*', pp. 81–110. See also Pantin, *English Church*, pp. 195–202.

disorganised.[18] But Fr Boyle has argued convincingly that Davis's judgment rested on a misunderstanding of the tripartite division, which required the treatment of similar issues from different points of view. It was perhaps the best of the English manuals for parochial clergy; it evidently had the widest circulation,[19] and was the basis of penitential discipline in England for the next two centuries. It was also the basis of other books. Much of it was built into Richard Rolle's treatise of the 1320s, *Iudica me*,[20] and the anonymous *Regimen animarum* of 1343;[21] and a revised or rewritten version of the whole was produced in 1384 by John de Burgh, Chancellor of Cambridge University, under the title *Pupilla oculi*.[22] The first section of the *Oculus* is of greatest legal interest, since it answers questions of a legal or quasi-legal character: how to examine penitents; how to categorise offences; and the extent of a priest's authority to award penance or grant absolution. It is highly practical. For instance, when examining a penitent who has drunk too much, the priest is recommended to inquire into the reason for the drunkenness: whether it was because he did not know the power of wine, or because he was in the company of guests, or because of exceeding thirst. There is a detailed account of general and provincial legislation, and also of the excommunications attaching to violations of Magna Carta and the Carta de Foresta. Dr Pantin has rightly drawn attention to the constitutional interest of this last feature: that fourteenth-century folk were supposedly kept informed about Magna Carta and

---

18 H. W. C. Davis, 'The Canon Law in England', *Zeitschrift der Savigny Stiftung für Rechtsgeschichte*, Kanonistische Abteilung, 34 (1913), p. 344, at pp. 349–50.

19 Boyle lists over fifty surviving manuscripts.

20 Pantin, *English Church*, p. 248.

21 Ibid., p. 203.

22 This was printed in 1510, by William Hopyl for William Bretton, as *Pupilla oculi omnibus presbyteris precipue Anglicanis*.

other legislation by their parish priest.[23] The *Dextera pars*, though concerned with pastoral matters, was also heavily based on canon law and included a rather alarming list of automatic excommunications.

The 'Mirror of Prelates' (Speculum praelatorum) was an even larger and perhaps over-ambitious reference work, incorporating portions of the *Oculus* and *Summa summarum*. In addition it provided sermon outlines for every Sunday and other liturgical occasions, and a dictionary of quotations from the Fathers. It seems not to have circulated widely: in fact only one complete manuscript is known.[24] But parts of it circulated separately in the form of tracts for the guidance of archdeacons and of monks and friars (*Speculum religiosorum*).[25]

Finally, we may notice the 'Mirror of King Edward III' (*Speculum regis Edwardi Tercii*).[26] This has been printed, though in a somewhat inaccessible edition.[27] It was an expanded version of a letter of protest, called the *Epistola ad Regem Edwardum*, setting out the grievances of the people in the neighbourhood of Windsor Forest against arbitrary abuses of the prerogative of purveyance by the King's commissioners. This prerogative, which caused resentment and discontent throughout the centuries until its repeal in 1645,[28] enabled ministers to commandeer provisions and labour in the King's name, usually without immediate payment, and often without payment at all. The tract is not merely an

23 Ibid., p. 198.
24 At Merton College, Oxford: Boyle, 'The *Oculus sacerdotis*', pp. 97–98, 102; idem 'The *Summa summarum*', pp. 432–33, 454. It was not a unique text, because William of Wykeham left a copy to New College; 'The *Summa summarum*', p. 434 n. 99.
25 There is a manuscript of this latter in Gray's Inn library (MS 11). Boyle lists five other manuscripts.
26 L. E. Boyle, 'William of Pagula and the *Speculum Regis Edwardi III*', *Mediaeval Studies*, 32 (1970), pp. 329–36.
27 J. Moisant, ed., *De speculo regis Edwardi III* (Paris, 1891), pp. 83–123.
28 Act of the Long Parliament, re-enacted by 12 Car. II, c. 24.

eloquent grumble; it makes use of legal arguments and is evidently the work of a canon lawyer. It was formerly attributed to Archbishop Simon Islip († 1366): indeed, Sir Edward Coke owned a copy attributed to Islip, and so cited it in the *Institutes*.[29] Professor Tait attributed it, in 1901, to Archbishop Simon Mepham († 1333).[30] But the letter is clearly by Paull, whose cure was near Windsor, and Fr Boyle argues that the *Speculum* is a recension by the same author. Apart from the close connection between the two texts, he has found what appear to be early references to a treatise *ad regem* expressly attributed to Paull.

It is easy for our age, largely cut off from its Latin heritage, to dismiss the writings of a fourteenth-century parish priest as irrelevant to the general course of human progress. But oblivion is sometimes the result of mere bibliographical accident. Dr Pantin said of Paull that he was 'one of the few outstanding canonist writers that later medieval England produced, comparable in his way to John Acton or Lyndwood':

> He seems to be the first writer of a manual for English parish clergy to make use of the local English legislation, such as the constitutions of the thirteenth-century papal legates and Archbishops of Canterbury ... He is remarkable for combining a mastery of canon law with a genuine interest in pastoral theology and a desire to improve the cure of souls; he reminds us that we cannot always put 'theologians' and 'canonists' into separate, watertight compartments, and that we must not dismiss the canonists as a race of soulless administrators.[31]

---

29 2 Co. Inst. 545. It was still at Holkham Hall in 1932: see W. O. Hassall, ed., *A Catalogue of the Library of Sir Edward Coke* (New Haven, 1950), p. 57, no. 700. It is there attributed to Islip.

30 J. Tait, 'On the Date and Authorship of the *Speculum Regis Edwardi*', *English Historical Review*, 61 (1901), pp. 110–15.

31 Pantin, *English Church*, p. 196.

3

William Bateman

ITH William Bateman († 1355) the study and practice of canon law in England received new encouragement and English canonists moved firmly onto the international stage. His influence was of a different kind from that exerted by most of the canonists remembered here. Many were the accomplished lawyers who led an active life in legal practice – or as 'soulless administrators' – without leaving any identifiable mark on history, but Bateman constitutes a remarkable exception to the usual pattern. Distinguished judge, leading figure in the Curia at Avignon and patron of legal studies in Cambridge, he left several marks on history which entitle him, though not known as an author, to be classed with the greatest English canon lawyers.

William Bateman was usually known to contemporaries as William of Norwich. He was the son of a leading citizen of that city, and must have been born a few years before 1300. He read law at Cambridge, taking the doctorate before 1328, the year in which he was appointed Archdeacon of Norwich. In 1340 he became Dean of Lincoln, but four years later returned to Norwich as bishop. He occupied the see until his death on 6 January 1355.[1] The list of his English

---

1 The biographical details are conveniently summarised in Emden, *Biographical Register of the University of Cambridge to 1500*, p. 44. A more minute account may be found in A. Hamilton Thompson, 'William Bateman, Bishop of Norwich, 1344–1355', *Norfolk Archaeology*, 25 (1935), pp. 102–37. See also *DNB*, i,

preferments is less indicative of his actual career than the fact that they were obtained by papal provision: they were, in other words, rewards for services elsewhere. His principal services were indeed rendered a great distance from Norwich and Lincoln. Only a year after his becoming an archdeacon, we find that he was appointed an 'auditor of the sacred apostolic palace' at Avignon. This meant that he was one of the judges of the Rota, the highest ecclesiastical court in western Christendom.[2] He is said to have achieved a position of high favour in the papal palace, both for his unblemished conduct and for his excellent learning, and to have been regarded by Pope John XXII and the whole Curia as the principal ornament of the legal profession ('utriusque iuris peritorum flos praecipuus'): no mean praise in those times for an English lawyer, if indeed it was the opinion prevalent in Avignon.[3] It is tempting to guess that he played a prominent part in the reorganisation of the Rota, which was given a settled constitution by the bull *Ratio iuris* of 1331 and thereafter entered upon a new phase of activity. The significance of this development was considerable, for it put the decisions of learned judges on a parallel footing with papal decretals and doctrinal writings as sources of canon law.[4]

Bateman's episcopal promotion put an end to his judicial activities, but not to his international career. He was employed by King Edward III on Anglo-French diplomatic

---

pp. 1315–16 (article by E. Venables).

2 For the Rota, see J. H. Baker, 'Dr Thomas Fastolf and the History of Law Reporting', *Cambridge Law Journal*, 45 (1986), pp. 84–96, at pp. 84–85, and the literature cited there.

3 The phrase is used in the contemporary *Vita Gulielmi Bateman* by Prior Lawrence of Norwich, which admittedly savours more of eulogy than biography; it is printed in F. Peck, *Desiderata curiosa* (1779), ii, p. 240.

4 See W. Ullmann, 'A Decision of the Rota Romana on the Benefit of Clergy in England', *Studia Gratiana*, 13 (1967), pp. 457–89.

GULIELMUS BATEMAN *Episcop. Norvic.*
Aulæ S.S. *et individuæ Trinitatis Fund.* AD MCCCL

William Bateman U.J.D. († 1355). Mezzotint by William Robins (1731), based on Bateman's private seal. The origin of this plate is explained in *Warren's Book*, ed. A.W.W. Dale (Cambridge, 1911), p. 10. The earlier mezzotint portrait of Bateman by John Faber (1714) is wholly fanciful.

missions throughout the 1340s and early 1350s, and as he was also engaged in the central affairs of the church he cannot have spent more than half his time – if that – in his diocese. Indeed he died in Avignon, and was buried there before the high altar in the cathedral, at a service conducted by the Patriarch of Jerusalem in the presence of all the resident cardinals.5

One consequence of his eminent status in the Curia was that he was able to surround himself in the palace with an entourage of English lawyers, most of them from East Anglia and probably from Cambridge.6 His influence is clearly apparent in the membership of the supreme ecclesiastical judiciary. After Bateman's appointment to the Rota, all the English auditors for a generation or two (1340–80) were East Anglians, either protégés of Bateman or at least Cambridge graduates associated with Bateman's foundations there: Thomas Fastolf of Yarmouth (later Bishop of St David's),7 Simon Theobald of Sudbury (later Archbishop of Canterbury),8 William of Lynn (later Bishop of Chichester), Thomas of Paxton, Robert of Stratton (first Master of Trinity Hall), Roger of Fritton, Richard Scrope (later Archbishop of York), Nicholas of Bottisham, and Thomas Theobald of Sudbury (Simon's brother).

5 There is no trace of any memorial.

6 For details, see Baker, 'Dr Thomas Fastolf', pp. 88–89, 95–96; Ullmann, 'A Decision of the Rota Romana', at pp. 466 et seq.

7 Fastolf was born in the Norwich diocese, but cannot certainly be connected with Cambridge. He had a licence to study in Italy in 1325–35, extended to 1339: Boyle, 'Canon Law before 1380', in *History of the University of Oxford*, i, p. 559 n. 1.

8 Sudbury studied law at Paris. He was murdered in 1381 on Tower Hill by the insurgents. See the life in *DNB*, xix, pp. 146–49.

420

DECISIONES

PER R· PATREM

THOMAM FASTOLI,

AVDITOREM SACRI PALATII,

IN VNVM REDACTAE.

CAVSA I.

ANNO Domini M. cccxxxvi. Pontificatus sanctissimi in Christo patris & domini, domini Benedicti Papæ xii. anno secundo die xi. mensis Decembris fuit in Rota propositū qd- dam negotium spoliationis per dominū Du- randum in quo lectum fuit quoddam instru- mentum productum ad spoliationem probã dum in illo negotio & ostendebatur quidam libellus siue petitio quædam super spoliatio- ne quædam facta per spoliatum lite penden- te:nec ibi exprimebatur quo tépore spolias- set, vtrum ante spoliationem factam de ipso, an post:& petebat reus huiusmodi se re- stitui, & id quod actum sic fuerat, retractari tanquam attentatum lite pendente . Circa præmissa autem mouebantur hęc dubia.

SVMMARIVM.

1 *Spoliatio an possit probari per instrumentum?*
2 *Crimen an possit probari per instrumentum?*

DVBIVM I.

1 PRimò † an spoliatio a posset probari per
2 instrumentum,& tenebatur quòd sic ar gu.extrà de restit.spol.c.cum ad sedem. ver. Nos prioris.& de ma.& obe.c.cum in eccle- sijs . licet ibi uideatur notari contrarium in 2 periurio.Et de hoc notatur, scilicet an † cri men per instrumétum posnt probari. per Io. And.de iureiur.c.fi.lib.6.& de uerbo.lignifi.

c.constitutionem.eod.lib.Item in iure ciui- li nota.ff.ad Turpil l. in senatus. & C. ad le- gem Aqui.l.contra negantem. prædictæ glo. omnes præter primam in decretali c. cum in ecclesijs,probant quod crimina possunt pro- bari per instrumentum.Goffred tamen pro- bat contrarium in uiolentia & possessione in summa de clandel.despon. uer.Illud autē no.& idem uidetur recitare Ioan.And. post Host.de excep.c pia.in gl.super uerbo 8.die- rum.circa fine.ibi, sed de spoliatione no. &c.

ADDITIO.

Spoliatio.Adde quod spoliatio probatur eo ipso,cp spoliatus probat de antiquiori possef sione.Bal.in l pen.col.vlti.C.si à non compe. iud.Alex.in l.si duo.ff.vti possi.

SVMMARIVM.

1 *Instrumentum in quo non apparet notarium esse rogatum,an valeat?*

DVBIVM II.

1 SEcundum dubium erat † an instrumentū valeat,si nõ appareret notarium esse roga tum,& tenebatur quod in dubio præsumeba tur ipsum esse rogatū:& hoc no.glo.in Auth. de tabel.§.nos autem credimus,super verbo iniungitur : contrarium videtur sentire Inn. extra de fide instrum c. r.ibi,non enim credi- mus,&c. & melius ibi.Ité no.vtile, &c. licet ibi simul referat alios ille in opinione contra ria,ibi,alij tamen,&c.

SVMMARIVM.

1 *Instrumentum in quo non cauetur, quòd spolia- tio sit facta nemine illius,cõtra quem ã atus fuit libellus,an probet?*

Ggg 4   DV-

Fastolf's reports, from *Decisiones novae, antiquae et antiquiores* (Venice, 1585), fo. 420r. Fastolf's cases were never printed in England, but were reprinted many times in continental collections of the decisiones rotae, of which this is one of the latest.

From a book in the possession of the author

Law Reporting

One of these papal judges, Dr Thomas Fastolf († 1361), enjoys the credit of being the first identifiable reporter of cases in the Rota.9 Although English common lawyers had begun reporting cases in the 1260s, the practice was not coeval in the Roman law tradition because of the different role which it attributed to the judge. It was not until the Renaissance period, with the creation of learned judicial tribunals, that a wave of law reports began to flood the Continent. The principal model for those continental royal courts was the papal court, with its professional judges, all doctors of law; and the principal model for the reporters in such courts was the series of *decisiones rotae* which began in the fourteenth century at Avignon. Of these, the first series in print is that compiled by Fastolf between December 1336 and February 1337. It was printed at Rome in 1475, and frequently reprinted thereafter. The reports are in Latin and give the facts of the cases and the arguments of the auditors, with the authorities cited. As with the English year books, the names of the speakers are given, and in several places Fastolf attributes views to one 'Dominus Willelmus', who must be our William of Norwich. As it happens, Fastolf's reports contain (in 1336) the first known use of the expression 'Rota', as a colloquial name for the apostolic Court of Audience, alluding to the wheel-shaped arrangement of the benches in the great hall of the palace ('La Grande Audience').10

Whether Fastolf was actually the first reporter is less than

9 For what follows, see Baker, 'Dr Thomas Fastolf'.
10 The impressive hall which still stands was rebuilt under Pope Clement VI (1342–52), and the court moved there in 1352: Baker, 'Dr Thomas Fastolf', p. 85. Fastolf's reference shows that the same arrangement obtained in the earlier hall, the foundations of which have been revealed by excavation. In neither hall is there any remaining trace of the circular seating.

clear; but, so far as present knowledge indicates, the initiation of reporting is undoubtedly to be associated with Bateman's circle of lawyers. There were evidently other English reporters at Avignon in the same period. A manuscript in Hereford Cathedral, almost certainly written by Simon of Sudbury († 1381), refers to opinions delivered by 'my lord of Norwich' ('dominus meus Norwycensis');[11] while a manuscript in New College, Oxford, contains notes of judgments by 'Dominus Willelmus de Norwyco' written by Richard Vaughan as King's Proctor at Avignon in 1339.[12]

Sudbury's reports are interesting for another reason. They contain cases, still unpublished, from the 1350s, several of which are of English provenance. One of the cases concerns the vicarage of Mildenhall, which was caught up in a five-year feud between Bateman as Bishop of Norwich and the Abbot of Bury St Edmunds.[13] But some at least of the material dates from before 1335 and is therefore older than Fastolf's printed reports. Since Sudbury refers in one place to *Repertorium domini*, and since his 'lord' was demonstrably Bateman ('dominus meus Norwycensis'), it is permissible to conjecture that this material came from Bateman himself. This possibility is strengthened by the knowledge that Bateman bequeathed to Trinity Hall a book containing 'many allegations and decisions of the doubts of the Roman Curia'.[14] Unfortunately, the manuscript has not

11 Hereford Cathedral, MS O. IV. 15: see G. Dolezalek, 'Quaestiones motae in Rota', in *Proceedings of the 5th International Congress of Medieval Canon Law* (Vatican City, 1980), p. 99, at pp. 104–5; Baker, 'Dr Thomas Fastolf', p. 93.

12 New College, Oxford, MS 207 (a copy of the *Sext*): see Boyle, 'The *Summa summarum*', p. 416.

13 For details, see Thompson, 'William Bateman', at pp. 118–21. The abbey won.

14 G. E. Corrie, 'A Catalogue of the Books Given to Trinity Hall, Cambridge, by the Founder' (1864), *Cambridge Antiquarian Society Communications*, 2, pp. 73–78, at p. 76.

survived, and so we cannot tell whether these were Bateman's own reports. But whatever part Bateman personally played in the beginning of law reporting in the Rota, the achievement of these Englishmen deserves to be remembered, especially in an age when English lawyers once more seek a place on the European legal scene. The reporters who followed their example, both in the Rota and in its secular counterparts, laid the foundations of a *ius commune* which was current throughout continental Europe before the Napoleonic period of codification. The case-law tradition which is so often supposed to isolate English law from the mainland was once seen as a means of legal harmonisation; and, had it prevailed in its older form, the foundation of canonistic law reporting by the forgotten East Anglian jurists of the fourteenth century would by now be hailed as a contribution of the first importance to European jurisprudence.

Bateman and Legal Studies in Cambridge

Bateman's second claim to fame is much better known, at any rate in Cambridge.[15] In 1350 he founded Trinity Hall, which he called 'The College of Scholars of the Holy Trinity of Norwich', and which he intended (in his own words) as a perpetual college of scholars of canon and civil law in the University of Cambridge, for the benefit and guidance of the common weal and especially of the diocese of Norwich. The founder's statutes were sealed in 1352.[16] There was to be a warden and up to twenty fellows – a long-term ambition not achieved under the original endowment

---

15 What follows is largely based on C. Crawley, *Trinity Hall: The History of a Cambridge College, 1350–1975* (Cambridge, 1976), pp. 1–16.

16 Printed in *Documents Relating to the University and Colleges of Cambridge* (Cambridge, 1852), ii, pp. 414–36.

– comprising ten to thirteen civilians and up to ten canonists. New fellows were to take an oath to promote the interests of the church of Norwich, and not to act professionally against the bishop or the chapter. Fellows were to converse in Latin, and to hold disputations upon a *quaestio* of canon or civil law three times a week, at which attendance was compulsory. They were to proceed to the doctorate within three years, receiving a present of £5 on so doing. Civilians were to proceed to the study of canon law; and canonists were to proceed to ordination, though they could remain fellows until they obtained benefices. There was to be a law library, to which Bateman himself contributed an impressive bequest of law books.[17] The first Master (from 1350 to 1355) was Robert of Stratton († 1380?), whom we have already noticed as an auditor of the Rota. His distinction was recognised by French and German law reporters who noted some of his judicial opinions.[18] Not only Stratton but three of the first fellows of the Hall were on Bateman's staff in Avignon at the time of his death. Cambridge law teachers were not meant to be cloistered monks.

The principal purpose of Bateman's first foundation seems to have been to supply the church with trained administrators and lawyers, preference being given to the needs of his own diocese, but with an eye on the wider world of legal affairs and diplomacy. The exclusive emphasis on legal studies within a college was unique in Cambridge. But Bateman's contribution to the establishment of a thriving law faculty in Cambridge did not end with Trinity Hall. He was also the second founder of Annunciation Hall, or Gonville Hall (now

17 Corrie, 'A Catalogue of the Books Given to Trinity Hall, Cambridge, by the Founder'. Only two can be identified now.

18 They appear in the printed *decisiones rotae*: Baker, 'Dr Thomas Fastolf', p. 89. Dr Stratton is not to be confused with Robert of Stretton († 1385), the illiterate Bishop of Lichfield; the mistake is made in H. E. Malden, *Trinity Hall* (1902), pp. 43–46.

Gonville and Caius College).[19] Edmund Gonville († 1351), a
Norfolk parson who had apparently made some money out
of property management, began to make plans for a Cambridge college in the late 1340s. He obtained a charter
licensing its foundation in 1348, but died before the plans
were brought to fruition. Gonville's draft statutes envisaged
a body of students of philosophy and theology, with law
apparently added as an afterthought – perhaps even as a
grudging exception. Bateman took over the project as Gonville's executor, saw the college founded, and in 1353
arranged an exchange of land which settled Gonville Hall on
its present site next to Trinity Hall.[20] He drew up statutes
of his own under which the fellows, if arts men, were now
enjoined to proceed to civil or canon law, theology or me-
dicine. The fellows were expected to come from the diocese
of Norwich, and no doubt many were expected to return to
its service. The parallels with Trinity Hall were marked by
a 'treaty of amity' which Bateman arranged between the two
societies.[21] The first Master, John Colton († 1404, later
Archbishop of Armagh and Chancellor of Ireland), was – like
Stratton of Trinity Hall – a canonist with service at Avignon.
Doubtless Bateman would have liked his second college also
to be well stocked with useful lawyers. The flimsy evidence
suggests that theology in fact predominated in the middle
ages, as Gonville would have wished. Yet Gonville Hall more
than earned its place in legal history by attracting William
Lyndwood around the end of the century.[22]

---

19 What follows draws heavily on C. Brooke, *A History of Gonville
and Caius College* (Woodbridge, 1985), pp. 1–19.
20 This released land near St Benet's Church for the newly founded
Corpus Christi College.
21 Bateman regarded Trinity Hall as the elder sister; but the university, having regard to the date of the charter, now treats Gonville
and Caius College as the senior.
22 Below, p. 44.

Canon Law and the Common Law

It is an interesting speculation whether Bateman was influenced by his general knowledge of the common-law system in making the various innovations mentioned above. The growing importance of judicial decisions, and the practice of reporting the discussions which led to those decisions, have obvious affinities with the system found in Westminster Hall. The common lawyer of today can identify more readily with the working system of canon law as glimpsed through Fastolf's reports than with the more abstract learning found in the traditional canonical texts. And there is a less obvious, but perhaps more instructive, parallel in the context of legal education. The decade of Bateman's educational foundations, with their emphasis on legal study, was the very decade in which, according to recent investigations, the inns of court were becoming settled residential law schools, with elaborate lectures and disputations embedded in the daily routine.[23] The teachers in the inns of court, as in Trinity Hall, were typically active and practical men destined for the bench and public service. For Bateman there was a direct link between academic legal study and judicial or public service in a supranational church. In his world the boundaries between English and foreign, between academic and practical, were at the deepest level insignificant.

23 The evidence is discussed in the introduction by J. H. Baker to *Readings and Moots at the Inns of Court in the Fifteenth Century*, ii, *Moots and Readers' Cases*, Selden Society, 105 (1990); and in idem, *The Third University of England: The Inns of Court and the Common-Law Tradition*, Selden Society lecture (1990).

4

John Ayton

N exact contemporary of Bateman, but distinguished by his words rather than his deeds, was John 'of Aton'. The name requires some comment before proceeding to the man. In the earliest printed edition of his work he is 'de Athon:' or 'de Aton', which Stubbs rendered as Ayton, on the assumption that the place intended was Ayton in Yorkshire.[1] He is likewise spelt Aton in other contemporary English manuscripts.[2] Maitland said it was convenient to follow the Ayton spelling, though he pointed out that the papal chancery addressed him as 'Johannes Johannis de Acton'.[3] 'Acton' was adopted in the *Dictionary of National Biography*,[4] and seems to have become the preferred spelling, though more cautious writers have adopted the neutral 'Athon'. In view of the strong East Anglian bias of the Cambridge law school in the time of Bishop Bateman, it is of course possible that the name derived from Acton in Suffolk. But that is only so if the remote papal chancery may be trusted; Athona is hardly a variant of Acton. If, on the other hand, the spelling 'Aton' in the treatise and in contemporary manuscripts is preferred, Ayton remains a

---

1 The place was formerly spelt Aton: E. Ekwall, *The Concise Oxford Dictionary of English Place-Names* (4th edn, Oxford, 1960), p. 21. A less likely possibility is Eaton.
2 See below, pp. 30, 32 n. 12.
3 F. W. Maitland, *Roman Canon Law in the Church of England* (Cambridge, 1898), p. 6.
4 Article by Sir Sidney Lee, *DNB*, i, p. 67.

more likely identification than any other. Certainly the doctor's connections in his professional career seem to have been with the north rather than with East Anglia.

Ayton read canon law at Cambridge and was a doctor of both laws by 1335.5 He must therefore have been known to Bateman, though he does not seem to have moved in Bateman's gilded circle, and it may be that he spent a formative period at Oxford, where he was a pupil of John Stratford († 1348), sometime vice-chancellor of that university, a distinguished lawyer who served as Dean of the Arches before becoming Chancellor of England (1330) and Archbishop of Canterbury (1333). Ayton calls Stratford *doctor meus*, and apparently wrote his gloss soon after Stratford became archbishop.6 But it is clear that he went on to teach law at Cambridge, since one of the few surviving reports of a *quaestio* or law disputation there contains a debate between 'Johannes de Aton, doctor in decretis' and Walter Elveden in about 1330.7 It was probably around the time of his doctorate in canon law that Ayton began his celebrated commentary on the legatine constitutions: indeed, he referred to it twelve years later when recalling his days at Cambridge, 'lecturing, disputing, writing my gloss on the legatine constitutions, speaking with all the assurance of a man with a professorial chair at his back'.8 In between stints

5 For biographical details, see Emden, *Biographical Register of the University of Oxford*, i, p. 11; idem, *Biographical Register of the University of Cambridge*, p. 2. Ayton became a Canon of Lincoln in 1329, apparently before ordination, and was Rector of Willingham by Stow, Lincolnshire, from 1330 until his death.

6 Maitland, *Roman Canon Law in the Church of England*, p. 6.

7 Gonville and Caius College, Cambridge, MS 483, fo. 275r; cited by Boyle, 'The *Summa summarum*' (above, p. 10), at p. 417; Selden Society, 95, pp. xvii–xviii. The manuscript was left to the college, with a number of other books, by Elveden himself.

8 From his manuscript tract *Septuplum*, quoted by Boyle, 'The *Summa summarum*', p. 418.

John Ayton's *Constitutiones Angliae*, showing the title-page of the 1504 (Paris) edition.

By permission of Cambridge University Library

at Cambridge he served as Official of the Court of York, and he was in the service of the Bishop of Durham in the 1340s. The several references to York in his gloss suggest that he had lived there before completing it. He refers to a custom of York as to procedure, which 'seems to be confounded' by the text;[9] discusses the position of certain canons of York who received income from Beverley,[10] and refers to St Leonard's Hospital in York.[11]

Ayton is credited with a few unpublished works: *Septuplum* (written in 1346), which was a treatise on the seven deadly sins and on penance,[12] a *Summa justiciae*, and perhaps others.[13] But his fame rests on the substantial gloss which he compiled upon the legatine constitutions, the first

9 C. Otto, tit. 26, 'Tanto', gl. ad v. *Rescribere* [1504 edn, fo. 52v; 1679 edn, p. 65].

10 C. Ottobuono, tit. 29, 'Christiane', gl. ad v. *Pluralitatem* [1504 edn, fo. 99v; 1679 edn, p. 128].

11 C. Ottobuono, tit. 48, 'Volentes', gl. ad v. *Custodes hospitalium* [1504 edn, fo. 106v; 1679 edn, p. 150].

12 Boyle, 'The *Summa summarum*', p. 418. There are two manuscripts in Cambridge attributed to 'Aton': Gonville and Caius College, MS 282 ('Iohannis de Atona septuplum cum commento', copy dated 1355); Trinity College, MS B. 14.4 ('Septuplum Iohannis de Aton cum glossa eiusdem'). (Cf. University College, Oxford, MS 71; Eton College, MS 30; Lincoln Cathedral, MS A.2.1, which seem to be related.) See M. W. Bloomfield et al., *Incipits of Latin Works on the Virtues and Vices* (Cambridge, Massachusetts, 1979), p. 503, no. 5826, and p. 509, no. 5892.

13 An early note in Peterhouse, Cambridge, MS 255, ad fin., says he wrote *Septuplum*, a *Summa iusticiae*, and also a treatise called *Qui bene praesunt*: M. R. James, *Catalogue of the MSS in Peterhouse* (Cambridge, 1899), p. 321. *DNB* says there is a manuscript of the *Summa* in Corpus Christi College, Cambridge, but it is not to be found in James's catalogue. There are at least three medieval treatises found in England beginning *Qui bene praesunt*: see A. G. Little, *Initia operum latinorum* (Manchester, 1904), p. 195. In All Souls College, Oxford, MS 42, fo. 203v, are *Quaestiones et notabilia Iohannis Athonis*, beginning with a typical Ayton pun, 'Abbas est nomen oneris et non honoris'; this seems to be an alphabetical digest from the gloss.

John Ayton's *Constitutiones Angliae*, showing the half-title of the 1504 (Paris) edition.

By permission of Cambridge University Library

major treatise on Anglican canon law – if we may use that phrase without meaning, of course, the law of a separate church, but legislation peculiar to the church in England.[14] His text was the legislation promulgated at the councils held in London by the papal legates Otto (1237) and Ottobuono (1268).[15] The second of these series in particular, comprising fifty-three canons, 'became the most important single collection of local law for the English Church'.[16] The gloss likewise became a standard work, as is evident from the number of surviving manuscript copies. There can be no doubt about its authorship. Besides a prologue, in which 'I, John of Ayton, Canon of Lincoln', refers to himself deprecatingly as 'among doctors of both laws hardly worthy to use up sheets of parchment' ('inter utriusque iuris doctores vix dignus occupare membranes'), many of the individual notes are signed at the end with his name.

The glosses were first printed in Paris in 1504, in a beautiful edition which might well claim to be one of the most visually attractive law books ever published for use in England.[17] The main title-page has a large woodcut of St George and the Dragon, and bears the title *Constitutiones legitime seu legatine regionis anglicane cum subtilissima interpretatione domini Johannis de Athon:*. On the verso is a letter of dedication to William Warham, Archbishop of Canterbury, dated on the ides of September 1504 from the Parisian

---

14 There is a discussion in Ayton's gloss as to whether England for this purpose included Scotland: C. Otto, pr., 'Quoniam decet', gl. ad v. *Anglie* [1504 edn, fo. 4r; 1679 edn, p. 5]; C. Ottobuono, pr., 'Mandata', gl. ad v. *Scotie* [1504 edn, fo. 61v; 1679 edn, p. 79].

15 For this legislation, see F. M. Powicke and C. R. Cheney, *Councils and Synods Relating to the English Church*, ii, *1205–1313* (Oxford, 1964), pp. 238–40, 738–43.

16 Ibid., p. 739. The Latin text occupies pp. 747–92.

17 Description based on the CUL copy (Sel. 3.126^2). In these descriptions the punctuation and capitalisation have been modernised.

John Ayton's *Constitutiones Angliae*, showing the incipit on the second leaf of the 1506 edition. The text begins with a gloss on *Quoniam decet*, the preface to the legatine constitutions of Otto (1237).

By permission of Cambridge University Library

shop of Josse Bade (Jodocus Badius Ascensius). The letter
refers to editorial work by Jean Chapuys (Johannes Cha-
pusus), and the printers are identified both in the letter and
in the colophon as Wolfgang Hopyl and Johannes Confluen-
tius. After this leaf there follow, on fifteen unnumbered
leaves, a *triplex tabella* comprising: (1) a table of the subjects
in Ayton's gloss; (2) a table to Chapuys' notes; and (3) a
table of the incipits of the constitutions. There is then a
half-title, printed within two chained circles supported by
hawks: *Constitutiones legitime ecclesie totiusque regionis
anglicane ab legatis a latere summorum pontificum collecte
et a domino Johanne de Aton diligenter explanate. Divinum
opus omnibus iis qui sacris iniciati sunt: utile ac necessarium.*
The text of the work occupies 120 numbered folios, printed
with the gloss set around the text in black-letter type, with
rubrics, paragraph-marks and headlines in red; it is followed
(folios 121r–155r) by the unglossed text of some provincial
constitutions of the Archbishops of Canterbury from Lang-
ton to Islip.

Another edition was produced by Hopyl in 1506, for sale
in London by the publisher William Bretton and by booksel-
lers in St Paul's Churchyard at the signs of the Holy Trinity
(Henry Jacobi) and St Anne (Joyce Pelgrim).[18] This has a
different title-page, with a coat of arms supported by unicorns,[19] and the date of the letter of dedication is altered to

---

18 Description from the copy in St Catharine's College Library,
   Cambridge (H. II. 27²). This has the ownership inscription 'Ricardus Cowall Anno Domini 1527'. The foliation in this edition
   is very irregular and renders the tables nearly useless.
19 According to E. G. Duff, *A Century of the English Book Trade*
   (1905), p. 18, these are Bretton's arms. They may have been intended (in error) for Lyndwood's: below, p. 49. But they also
   occur in Bretton's 1510 edition of Burgh's *Pupilla oculi* (above,
   p. 13). Cf. R. B. McKerrow, *Printers' and Publishers' Devices in
   England and Scotland, 1485–1640* (1913), p. 7, no. 18 (no confir-
   matory evidence that they are Bretton's).

1506.[20] The half-title is also different, with woodcuts of the Trinity and the Fathers; it is inscribed, *Legatine seu constitutiones legitime cum summariis atque justis annotationibus politissimis characteribus summaque accuratione rursum revise atque impresse* ... *Venales habentur London' apud bibliopolas in cimiterio Sancti Pauli in signo Sanctissime Trinitatis et Sancte Anne matris Marie.* These editions, though bibliographically distinct, were now uniform with editions of Lyndwood's *Provinciale*;[21] and Ayton was subsequently reprinted only as an appendix to that work. The latest edition (of both Lyndwood and Ayton) was printed at Oxford in 1679, and reprinted in facsimile from that edition in 1968; this edition is the easiest to use, since the abbrevations were extended and some punctuation introduced.

Ayton cites a great many texts of the canon and civil laws, in the usual manner of the time. He is up to date, with frequent references to the *Extravagantes* of Pope John XXII († 1334), and to the glossator Johannes Andreae († 1348). Though he makes little use of case-law, he does refer to a decision of the Rota against the Prior and Canons of St Bartholomew's, Smithfield.[22] The legal authors most frequently cited are Andreae, Guy[do de Baysio] († 1313), occasionally cited as 'Archidiaconus', Hostiensis († 1271), Innocentius [Innocent IV] († 1254), and W. (probably William Durand, † 1296); there are also multiple references to Accursius († 1263), Barth[olomeus] Brix[iensis] († *c.* 1258), Ber[nardus de Parma] († 1266),[23] [Bernardus] Compostellanus (fl. 1200), Goffredus [de Trano] († 1245), Johannes

---

20 The text of this version is printed in P. Renouard, *Bibliographie des impressions et des oeuvres de Josse Badius Ascensius* (Paris, 1908), ii, pp. 52–53.

21 Below, p. 49.

22 C. Otto, tit. 6, 'Sacer ordo', gl. ad v. *Titulo* [1504 edn, fo. 9r; 1679 edn, p. 17]: 'Et sic fertur determinatum per omnes auditores palatii contra religiosos Sancti Bartholomei London'.

23 Some citations are 'secundum beatum Bernardum'.

Monachus [Jean le Moigne] († 1313), also cited as Cardinalis, and Raymundus [de Peñafort] († 1275). There are in addition references to the Bible, the Fathers, and to various classical and medieval authors. For example, in a discussion of sexual misbehaviour, Ayton prays in aid such diverse authorities as Horace, Ovid, St Jerome and Giraldus Cambrensis.[24] And in discussing whether it is good to make vows, he assembles the opinions of Saints Thomas Aquinas, Isidore, Anselm and Augustine.[25] However, as Maitland warned,[26] there are in the received text a number of obvious interpolations from later authors, and some caution is therefore necessary in distinguishing Ayton from later accretions. Ayton seems to have had little awareness of the secular law of England, or of English history, for he identifies a reference to English legislation in the Constitutions of Ottobuono (1268) as the Statute of Gloucester (1278), referring also to Westminster II (1285).[27] There is, nevertheless, an interesting interpretation of the words 'salvis domini regis privilegiis' as exempting the clerks of the Chancery from ecclesiastical sanctions for issuing writs of prohibition.[28]

Maitland was not very impressed by Ayton's work: 'I should suppose that John of Ayton was very much Lyndwood's inferior in all those qualities and acquirements that make a great lawyer. He is a little too human to be strictly scientific. His gloss often becomes a growl ...' He gives as

24 C. Otto, tit. 16, 'Licet ad profugandum', gl. ad v. *Contagium* [1504 edn, fo. 34r; 1679 edn, pp. 41–42]. The citation to Giraldus Cambrensis is 'Geraldus Menevensis archidyaconus li. de salubri exhortatione ad continentiam'.

25 C. Ottobuono, tit. 8, 'Quam indecorum', gl. ad v. *Professionis vinculo* [1504 edn, fo. 72v; 1679 edn, p. 93].

26 Maitland, *Roman Canon Law in the Church of England*, p. 7.

27 C. Ottobuono, tit. 23, 'Cum mortis', gl. ad v. *Cum approbatione regis* [1504 edn, fo. 95r; 1679 edn, p. 122].

28 C. Ottobuono, tit. 6, 'Cum honestatis', gl. ad v. *Privilegiis* [1504 edn, fo. 70v; 1679 edn, p. 91].

an example Ayton's impish derivation of the word 'official'
from the Latin *officio* (to obstruct).29 Fr Boyle, on the other
hand, described the gloss as 'magnificent'.30 The middle way
is to see Ayton as first and foremost a teacher. Although it
is unlikely that the work originated in lectures, it is written
in the idiom of the classroom; and, as a law teacher, Ayton
knew that a few lively examples could make a point more
effectively than a string of abstract principles ('Longum sit
iter per precepta, breve tamen et efficax per exempla').31
The teacher indulges his humour, and his fondness for ap-
posite classical aphorisms,32 and tries to inculcate legal logic
without losing the student's attention by putting forward
the occasional provocative conclusion. For instance, a constitution of Otto ordered that clergy should not keep
concubines publicly in their houses, but should discard them
within a month. This provides an opportunity to make some
good lawyer's points about the construction of legislation –
points calculated, no doubt, to shock the hearers into active
thought. Dr Ayton points out that the constitution does not
extend to clergy who keep concubines privately (*secrete*),
whether in their own houses or elsewhere; that being seen
a few times in public with a concubine is insufficient proof
of public keeping; and also that the penalty is avoided if a
clerk keeps a concubine off and on for a year or more,
provided he never keeps her for a whole month at a time.33
Here we might accuse our glossator of being too 'strictly

---

29 Maitland, *Roman Canon Law in the Church of England*, pp. 9–10.
30 Boyle, 'The *Summa summarum*', p. 418.
31 C. Otto, tit. 22, 'Quid ad venerabiles', gl. ad v. *In exemplum* [1679
   edn, p. 56]. Ayton is here quoting from Seneca: see L. A. Seneca,
   Ad Lucilium epistulae morales, ed. L. D. Reynolds (Oxford, 1965),
   i, p. 11, line 6.
32 He is fond in particular of Seneca, and cites his letters to Lucilius
   in several places: e.g. last note; below, p. 41 n. 43.
33 C. Otto, tit. 16, 'Licet ad profugandum', gl. ad v. *Detinent, Pub-
   lice, Concubinas* [1504 edn, fo. 35r-v; 1679 edn, pp. 43–44].

scientific' in his literal approach to legislative meaning, and indeed an eighteenth-century clergyman saw this passage as 'a great demonstration of the looseness of that Age, and especially of the Canonists';[34] but more likely we see a professor deriving some amusement from the timeless problem of loose or unduly narrow draftsmanship. Elsewhere, Ayton favours an equitable construction: for instance, where clergy are forbidden to wear (*portare*) coifs, he allows that *portare* should not be construed to include carrying them in a purse for use at night.[35]

In addition to his legal learning, Ayton provides some sidelights on contemporary English usages and manners: for instance, he notes that a penitent could show reverence to the priest at confession by doffing his hat and bowing, without necessarily genuflecting.[36] Whatever the older opinions, we are told that baptism must now be performed in the name of the Father, the Son and the Holy Ghost, and not merely in the name of the Trinity or in the name of Christ.[37] Ayton states that although priests were supposed to have a larger tonsure than deacons, this was not the current practice;[38] but he does argue that *tonsura honesta* implicitly requires shaving off the beard, 'which certain modern clerics eagerly cultivate with abominable freedom, contrary to law'.[39] In speaking of

34 J. Johnson, *A Collection of All the Ecclesiastical Laws* (1720), ii, sig. L2v. For Johnson, see below, p. 106.
35 C. Ottobuono, tit. 5, 'Cum sancti', gl. ad v. *Portare* [1504 edn, fo. 68v; 1679 edn, p. 88].
36 C. Ottobuono, tit. 2, 'Quoniam ceca', gl. ad v. *Cum reverentia* [1679 edn, p. 82]: 'capitium deponendo, genuflectendo, vel saltem inclinando'.
37 C. Otto, tit. 3, 'Ad baptismum', gl. ad v. *Exponant* [1504 edn, fo. 9r; 1679 edn, p. 11].
38 C. Otto, tit. 14, 'Quoniam de habitu', gl. ad v. *Decentes* [1504 edn, fo. 30v; 1679 edn, p. 37].
39 C. Otto, tit. 14, 'Quoniam de habitu', gl. ad v. *Tonsuram* [1504 edn, fo. 30v; 1679 edn, p. 37]: 'quam moderni quidam clerici abominabiliter prolixam nutriunt studiose contra legem'.

the excessive shortness of clothes, Ayton gives as an example the fashions worn by the gentry of his day, barely covering the knees.40 And of 'ridiculous' clothing, he opines that this refers to the dress of actors, comics and fools, which was especially designed to make men smile or laugh;41 and then tells the story of someone 'inordinately disguised' at a great joust, who was asked in reproachful terms, 'Sir, whose fool are you?' and replied, 'I am the fool of the abbot of the monastery of the Blessed Mary of York'.42 Yet, if Ayton was not much impressed by changing fashions, he was no ascetic either. He obviously valued humour, and he admitted to valuing good companionship: for 'nothing is worth having without friends to share it'.43

Although Ayton's style of exposition might be characterised as 'legalistic' in the least attractive sense of that term, the whole book is designed to stimulate the mind. The book even ends with a riddle, which no one has yet solved:44 'Hoc itaque presens meum opusculum in significatione triplici istarum figurarum 9, 2, 9, 5, 4, laboriose descriptum tam

40 C. Ottobuono, tit. 5, 'Cum sancti', gl. ad v. *Brevitate nimia* [1504 edn, fo. 68v; 1679 edn, p. 88]: 'ad modum forte armigerorum nostri temporis diversimode pompantium vix usque ad poplices'.

41 C. Ottobuono, tit. 5 'Cum sancti', gl. ad v. *Ridiculosas* [1679 edn, p. 88]: 'exemplo histrionis ioculatoris vel fatui quales proprie ad hominis risum et derisum parantur'.

42 Ibid.: 'Unde ad immensam burdam astantium fertur quendam fatuum uni magnati inordinate degysato sic anglice improperasse domine cuius stolidus estis vos: ego enim sum stolidus Abbatis Monasterii Beate Marie Eborum.'

43 C. Ottobuono, tit. 41, 'Monachos', gl. ad v. *Periculosum* [1679 edn, p. 147]: 'Nullius boni sine socio quasi omnimoda est possessio'). This is a borrowing from Seneca, *Ad Lucilium epistulae morales*, ed. Reynolds, i, p. 10, lines 26–27 ('nullius boni sine socio iucunda possessio est').

44 The writer is indebted to Dr Catherine Pickstock of Emmanuel College for introducing him to the mystic significance of numbers for medieval theologians. Her pupil nevertheless struggles in vain to understand Ayton's 'triple signification'.

scolares quam practici benigne si placet acceptent'.45 It must be centuries since Ayton's efforts were accessible to the generality of *practici*. Unlikely to find a modern editor, it is sad that its almost impenetrable abbreviated Latin should now protect it so inviolably from being read by more than a tiny and dwindling body of *scolares*.

45 'Peroratio domini Ioannis Athonensis' [1504 edn, fo. 120v; 'Peroratio Domini Johannis de Athona' in 1679 edn, p. 155].

5

William Lyndwood

ATEMAN's canonists had exerted their greatest influence at Avignon, and it may be no accident that the decline of English legal influence on the papal world, when it shifted from Avignon back to Rome, seems to have coincided with the strengthening of a canonistic presence in London. Although the formation of the informal society known as Doctors' Commons has been tentatively traced to a fellowship living in Paternoster Row near St Paul's in the 1490s,[1] there is little doubt that there was a community of canonists in London throughout the fifteenth century. A series of monumental inscriptions formerly in the Greyfriars, London, including at least seven 'advocates of the Canterbury Court of Arches' dying between 1400 and 1490,[2] is suggestive of some kind of communal life, as is the bequest by Dr Thomas Kent († 1469) of a library of civil and canon law books to be housed in London for use by the judges, advocates and proctors of the

---

1 G. D. Squibb, *Doctors' Commons* (Oxford, 1977), pp. 1–22. In 1496 the Proctors of Cambridge University paid for a dinner 'apud Pater Noster Row cum doctoribus de arcubus': ibid., p. 6. The doctors left the building in Paternoster Row in 1568, and it was destroyed in the Great Fire of London.
2 John Stow's church notes, BL, MS Harley 544, fos 50v–55v. The earliest was Stephen Sylk († 4 December 1400), 'advocatus curie Cant. ', and the latest James Hulton († 7 August 1490), 'advocatus curie Cant. de archubus'. There was also a register († 1484) and a proctor († 1428).

Arches.3 Another sign of this more domestic professional focus, perhaps, was the appearance of a great book on English canon law by the best known of all medieval English canonists, William Lyndwood, compiler of the glossed *Provinciale*.4

Lyndwood's name derives from what is now Linwood, in Lincolnshire, where his father John († 1419) was a woolman, and where (according to his will) he was born. William was sent to Cambridge, where he studied at Gonville Hall and is said to have become a Fellow of Pembroke Hall. In the old library of Gonville and Caius College there was an inscription in the window requesting prayers for Lyndwood as 'huius collegii quondam commensalis'. His lectures have not survived,5 and the exact dates of his university residence are not known,6 but he was certainly a doctor of both laws by 1407, when he was ordained priest. By that time he

---

3 PCC 26 Godyn; Emden, *Biographical Register of the University of Oxford*, ii, p. 1038. The testator called for a library to be built near St Paul's, but there is no evidence that this request was carried out. The library was to be open to other doctors and bachelors of law.

4 Biographical details from *DNB*, xii, pp. 340–42 (article by J. M. Rigg); Emden, *Biographical Register of the University of Cambridge*, pp. 379–81; A. Compton Reeves, 'The Careers of William Lyndwood', in *Documenting the Past*, ed. J. S. Hamilton and P. J. Bradley (Woodbridge, 1989), pp. 197–216. A book by Mgr Brian Ferme was published after this chapter was written, but was still not available in Cambridge at the time of revision: *Canon Law in Late Medieval England: A Study of William Lyndwood's Provinciale with Particular Reference to Testamentary Law*, Studia et Textus Historiae Iuris Canonici, 8 (Rome, 1996).

5 They are cited in W. Lyndwood, *Provinciale* (Oxford, 1679), p. 299, gl. ad v. *Fore praestanda* ('Hanc materiam tetigi in Lectura Decretorum 22, q. 1 in prin.'). All citations below to Lyndwood are to the 1679 edition.

6 Some writers speculate that his doctorate was from Oxford, though there is no direct evidence one way or the other. He did leave a law book to Oxford, but also left two to Cambridge.

already held a number of benefices – the earliest we know of was the wardenship of a hospital in 1396 – and he was to collect many more in the course of his career. As in Bateman's case, these were not actual occupations, but sources of income intended to maintain a lawyer destined for high office.

In 1414 Lyndwood became Chancellor of the Archbishop of Canterbury and Auditor of Causes, and three years later Official Principal of the Court of Arches. In the 1420s he served as prelocutor of the clergy in five convocations,[7] and was heavily involved in the proceedings against the Lollards: even a man of fine learning could not shrink from roasting his fellow men.[8] In the following decade

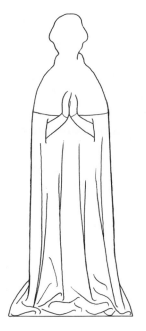

William Lyndwood LL.D. († 1446), wearing the habit of a doctor of laws. Drawing of the defaced figure on his father's brass (1419) at Linwood, Lincolnshire.

he became more frequently employed in the royal service. Prominent civilians were regularly commissioned to undertake diplomatic service overseas, and Lyndwood proved an invaluable envoy, representing the King in France, Holland, Flanders, Prussia and Portugal; he was King's Proctor at the Council of Basel in 1433. Like other civilians, he also acted from time to time as a commissioner to hear Admiralty

7 He mentions one such occasion (Lyndwood, *Provinciale*, p. 192, gl. ad v. *Provinciam*), when it was decided to replace the word 'archbishopric' in a canon with 'province'.

8 Lyndwood mentions Lollardy in *Provinciale*, pp. 284 and 300, and the penalty for heresy at p. 293.

causes.⁹ During the same period he became active in the central bureaucracy as Keeper of the Privy Seal (1432–43), and was
involved in the founding of Eton College and King's College,
Cambridge.¹⁰ His ultimate reward, which he enjoyed for only
four years, was the bishopric of St David's, obtained in 1442.
He died on 21 October 1446 and was buried in the chantry
of Our Lady of Pew in St Stephen's Chapel, Westminster. A
body with a crozier, thought to be his, was discovered in the
crypt in 1852 and reinterred in Westminster Abbey. The only
contemporary portrait of Dr Lyndwood is the worn figure
on his father's brass at Linwood, where the fourth son is
shown in the academical habit of a doctor of law.¹¹

The Provinciale

Lyndwood was clearly a figure of importance in the first
half of the Henry VI's reign, but even such an impressive
curriculum vitae would not have ensured his fame with
posterity. His claim to recognition as a pre-eminent canonist
rests on the *Provinciale*, his glossed edition of the conciliar
and synodal legislation of the province of Canterbury from
1222 down to his own time.¹² According to the preface, he

9 Reeves, 'The Careers of William Lyndwood', pp. 206, 207, 213.
10 As a colleague and protégé of Archbishop Chichele, he may also
   have been involved in some way with the foundation of All Souls
   College, Oxford.
11 Reproduced in *Monumental Brass Society Portfolio*, series 1, part
   8, plate 3; J. Page-Phillips, *Children on Brasses* (1970), fig. 7. He
   is wearing the LL.D. congregation habit with two arm-slits, hood
   and round cap; but the upper third of the figure has become worn
   almost flat. There is a fanciful woodcut portrait in pontifical dress
   in the 1496 edition of *Provinciale*: below, p. 49.
12 The principal studies are F. W. Maitland, *Roman Canon Law
   in the Church of England* (1898), ch. 1 (pp. 1–50); C. R. Cheney,
   'William Lyndwood's *Provinciale*', *The Jurist*, 21 (1961), pp. 405–
   34, reprinted in idem, *Medieval Texts and Studies* (1973),
   pp. 158–84.

Prouicialis wilhelmi lyndewode

A page from Lyndwood's *Provinciale*, showing part of the first title of Book IV, concerning marriage. The initial text is a constitution of the Council of Oxford 1322 concerning the proclamation of banns in church. In the first column, Lyndwood expounds the distinction between espousals and matrimony. From the first printed edition (Paris, 1501), folio 147v.

By permission of Cambridge University Library

had begun this work at the request of Archbishop Chichele. By 1422 he had completed the editorial work on the legislative texts, and from 1423 he began to devote his spare time to preparing the gloss. The main work was completed in 1430; and finally, on 25 January 1434, Lyndwood was able to sign off the index, where his name is curiously Latinised as 'Gulielmus de Tylia Nemore' (meaning linden wood, or lime grove). Like many successful law books, Littleton and Blackstone among them, the *Provinciale* purported to have been intended as much for inexpert readers as for lawyers. It was written, said Lyndwood, for those more concerned with the provincial legislation than with the general law of the church;[13] and it seems he had particularly in mind the lesser clergy, such as rural deans ('who are commonly unlearned and ignorant of law')[14] and archdeacons. Nevertheless, it abounds in citations and was hardly a nutshell guide for the beginner. In fact, it belonged within an established learned tradition. The idea of collecting canons and adding a commentary was nothing new in the Christian legal world, and there was an English model in Ayton's book on the legatine canons of Otto and Ottobuono.[15] In its own field, however, Lyndwood's work had no competitor, and it circulated very widely in manuscript.[16]

The *Provinciale* was one of the first law books printed in

---

13 Lyndwood, *Provinciale*, p. 95, gl. ad v. *Commenta* ('praesens opus non praecipue nec principaliter viris scribo scientia literarum preditis, sed potius simpliciter literatis et pauca intelligentibus, quorum labor, ut plurimum, magis assuescit in inspiciendis constitutionibus provincialibus quam aliis ecclesiae constitutionibus generalibus').

14 Lyndwood, *Provinciale*, p. 79 [C. Oxon., tit. 25], 'In causis', gl. ad v. *Audire* ('Ratio huius constitutionis potuit esse, quia, ut communiter, tales decani rurales sunt imperiti, et iuris ignari').

15 See above, pp. 32–33.

16 Cheney, 'Lyndwood's *Provinciale*', lists fifty-seven manuscripts in an appendix.

England, appearing around 1483 – two years after Littleton – under the imprint of Theodoric Rood of Oxford. This first edition has no title-page or date, but ends 'Explicit opus ... super constitutiones provinciales'.[17] It was next reprinted in Paris in 1501 and 1505, and at Antwerp in 1525, these continental editions (intended mainly for England) having Ayton's work appended.[18] The Parisian editions have a fine woodcut with the supposed arms of Lyndwood, *A fess crenelly between three fleurs de lys*,[19] quartering, *Crusilly a unicorn salient* (?Donne), supported by unicorns. The version of the *Provinciale* most commonly used today is that printed in Oxford by the university printer in 1679.[20]

There were also several printed editions of the constitutions alone, without the gloss. The first of these was printed at Caxton's shop by Wynkyn de Worde in 1496, with the title *Constitutiones provinciales ecclesie anglicane per d. Wilhelmum Lyndewode utriusque iuris doctorem edite. Incipiunt feliciter* [woodcut of a bishop, presumably meant to represent Lyndwood] *Opus presens fabricatum est et diligenter correctum per Wynandum de Worde. Apud Westmonasterium. In domo Caxston. Anno Incarnacionis millesimo quadragentesimo nonagesimo sexto. Ultima die May acabatumque gloria deo.* It was twice reprinted in 1499 (by de Worde, and separately by Pynson), around 1505 (by Pynson), in 1508, 1517,

17 There is a variant of this edition with much of the type reset: see G. Chawner, *A List of the Incunabula in the Library of King's College, Cambridge* (Cambridge, 1908), pp. 52–53.

18 See above, p. 37.

19 Cf. J. W. Papworth, *Ordinary of British Armorials* (1874), p. 754 ('Arg. a fess crenelly betw. three fleurs-de-lis sa. Lyndwood'). The Lyndwood brass of 1419 at Linwood, however, shows the arms as *A chevron between three linden leaves*: ibid., p. 454. It is possible that the arms in the woodcut are intended to be those of the printer William Bretton: above, p. 36 n. 19.

20 The date on the title-page. The explicit (p. 356) is dated 5 id. Jul. 1678, and identifies the publisher as Richard Davis. Ayton's book was included in the same volume, with a separate pagination.

1526 and 1529 (all by de Worde), and in 1557 (by Marshe).
Clearly the compilation remained in steady demand, at least
until the Reformation. In 1534 Redman published an English
translation of this edition, still unfortunately without the
gloss,[21] doubtless to meet lay demand following the parliamentary legislation which promised a revision of the canon
law.[22] The next edition was produced as late as 1664, in
duodecimo, by Dr Robert Sharrock († 1684) of New College,
Oxford, a civilian and divine who was also (according to
Anthony à Wood) 'very knowing in vegetables'.[23]

Professor Cheney has shown that Lyndwood's text of the
constitutions was, by modern standards of editing, and for
modern historical purposes, quite inadequate. Nothing earlier than 1222 is included; there are false attributions,
apocrypha, errors of transcription and even some apparently
deliberate changes of wording.[24] The historical conclusion,
however, should not be that Lyndwood was sloppy, but that
editions of our kind were simply not called for in his time.
The quality of Lyndwood's collection indeed closely re-
sembles that of the contemporary manuals of parliamentary
statutes, which exclude pre-1225 legislation from the canon,
incorporate apocrypha and abound with textual variations.
What was needed, in both systems, was a working reference
manual of current law; and no one worried too closely about

---

21 *Constitutions Provincialles, and of Otho, and Octhobone, Translated in to Englyshe* (1534). It was reprinted in 1929 as *Provinciale:
   The Text of the Canons Therein Contained*, ed. J. V. Bullard and
   H. C. Bell.
22 See below, p. 61.
23 *DNB*, xvii, p. 1368.
24 Cheney, 'Lyndwood's *Provinciale*', p. 176, instances an amendment to Winchelsey's decree concerning chancel repairs. The text
   stated simply that the responsibility rested on the rector, but
   Lyndwood interpolated the words *seu ad quos pertinent* so as to
   accommodate local customs (such as that of London) where the
   chancel belonged to the parishioners and was their responsibility.

chapter and verse. The material was not even reproduced in historical sequence,[25] but rearranged according to the topics in the Gregorian decretals. An edition of the modern kind was not available to scholars until 1717, when David Wilkins produced his *Concilia Magnae Britanniae*.[26]

Lyndwood's Contribution to Canon Law

The edition of the text of the provincial constitutions was of contemporary value as providing a corpus of English canons, though for the reasons given it is no longer of much use. The gloss, on the other hand, was and is far more valuable as a contribution to universal jurisprudence written from an English point of view. It was not intended as a complete textbook on English canon law, because the provincial legislation was not comprehensive. The English church was part of the universal church and governed by its common law (*ius commune*).[27] The main body of canon law, for England as for everywhere else, was the *Corpus iuris canonici*: what Lyndwood himself termed the *Corpus decretorum et decretalium*. For example, as Maitland pointed out, there was no English law of marriage formation; and so, for that subject, Lyndwood refers the reader to Innocent III and Johannes Andreae.[28] But the general law of the church allowed for regional legislation, and local custom, so that the church in England could lawfully adopt rules

---

25 This, also, is a feature of the manuscript *statuta vetera*.
26 Below, p. 111.
27 This canonical *ius commune*, unlike English common law, was largely written. The term *ius commune* is used in a slightly different sense by civilians. Cf. *Evers* v. *Owen* (1627) Godb. 431, at p. 432, *per* Dodderidge J. ('There is ... *Jus Commune Ecclesiasticum*, as well as *Jus Commune Laicum*').
28 Lyndwood, *Provinciale*, p. 271, gl. ad v. *Matrimonium*; Maitland, *Roman Canon Law in the Church of England*, p. 39. This was a gloss upon a constitution of Archbishop Walter Reynold (1322).

and practices supplementing or (occasionally) diverging from the general law, provided that they were not repugnant to it and could be justified by reasonableness and also – in the case of custom – by long usage.[29] Lyndwood's gloss was the principal guide to these English peculiarities, and was accepted as an authority throughout Christendom on the learning which accommodated them to the *ius commune*. Among these peculiarities were: (1) the treatment of defamation as a punishable offence, as a result of a constitution of the Council of Oxford (1222);[30] (2) the recognition of temporal jurisdiction over patronage, even though the universal canon law regarded this as spiritual;[31] (3) the jurisdiction of the church courts over probate,[32] and the recognition of local customs of succession;[33] (4) the liability of parishioners rather than rectors for nave repairs;[34] (5) the recognition of the Salisbury use as the liturgical norm in

29 See Maitland, *Canon Law in the Church of England*, pp. 19 et seq., 41–42.
30 C. Oxford, tit. 5, 'Excommunicamus', Lyndwood, *Provinciale*, pp. 346–47; F. M. Powicke and C. R. Cheney, ed., *Councils and Synods Relating to the English Church, 1205–1313* (Oxford, 1964), i, p. 107; R. H. Helmholz, *Select Cases on Defamation to 1600*, Selden Society, 101 (1985), pp. xiv–xli.
31 Ibid., p. 217, gl. ad v. *Foro regio* ('In quo tractatur causa iuris patronatus de consuetudine regni Angliae, licet pertineat ad forum ecclesiasticum secundum canones'), 316, gl. ad v. *Jure patronatus* ('licet causa iuris patronatus sit annexa spiritualibus, et sic pertineat ad forum ecclesiasticum ... consuetudo dat cognitionem foro temporali').
32 Ibid., p. 170, gl. ad v. *Insinuationem* ('Haec autem publicatio de consuetudine Angliae pertinet ad iudices ecclesiasticos ... Secus tamen est de iure communi'). He here cites authorities to the effect that jurisdiction may be enlarged by custom.
33 Ibid., p. 172, gl. ad v. *Consuetudinem patriae, Defunctos contingit*, and p. 178, gl. ad v. *Defunctum*.
34 Ibid., p. 53, gl. ad v. *Reparatione*, p. 250, gl. ad v. *Defectus ecclesiae*; ibid., p. 253, gl. ad v. *Navis ecclesiae*; J. H. Baker, 'Lay Rectors and Chancel Repairs', *Law Quarterly Review*, 100 (1984), p. 181.

England, contrary to the rule of the *ius commune* that the use of the metropolitical church should be observed;[35] and (6) the possibility of changing Christian names on confirmation.[36] For the most part, however, the emphasis is not on local divergence, and these English peculiarities occupy but a small place in the commentary. Lyndwood is generally at pains to show, by full citation of universally accepted legal authorities, how every word in the provincial legislation reinforces or supplements the catholic *ius commune*. Sometimes local legislation is dismissed as *ultra vires*, and even long usage is from time to time rejected. Usage cannot justify an improper divergence from explicit legislation, such as the lax English practice of permitting nuns to leave their cloisters for recreation, or to beg alms,[37] or a composition for tithes which might represent less than one tenth of income.[38] On the other hand, non-user of a particular constitution, if not scandalous or subversive of morals, might be sufficient to render it ineffective. Thus, although the Council of Oxford (1222) required rural deans and priests to wear the *cappa clausa*, this rule had fallen into disuse and was no longer binding.[39]

That Lyndwood's *Provinciale* became a standard work in his own lifetime is evident from his will, in which he directs

35 Ibid., p. 104, gl. ad v. *Usum Sarum Ecclesiae*. This is 'ex longa consuetudine'.

36 Ibid., p. 246, gl. ad v. *Corrigatur*. Cf. *Malom's Case* (1335) YB Pas. 9 Edw. III, fo. 14, pl. 18; Co. Litt. 3a.

37 Lyndwood, *Provinciale*, p. 212, gl. ad v. *Cum socia*; Maitland, *Canon Law in the Church of England*, pp. 27–31.

38 Ibid., p. 201, gl. ad v. *Negotiationum* (questioning a custom of London). Cf. ibid., p. 25, gl. ad v. *De consuetudine* (custom of England, laboriously defended).

39 Ibid., p. 118, [C. Oxford, tit. 33], 'Ut clericalis', gl. ad v. *Cappis clausis*. The *cappa clausa* was kept up only in the ancient universities, and vestiges of it (the scarlet 'cope' and the black proctor's 'ruff') may still be seen in Cambridge at congregations of the Regent House.

that the exemplar be kept chained in St Stephen's Chapel, Westminster, so that copyists might have recourse to it to correct their texts.[40] For the century following his death its popularity is attested by the number of manuscript copies and printed editions. Its authority was not directly affected by the restraint of appeals to Rome in 1534, because Parliament expressly enacted that 'such canons, constitutions, ordinances and synodals provincial being already made, which be not contrariant or repugnant to the laws, statutes and customs of this realm, nor to the damage or hurt of the King's prerogative royal, shall now still be used and executed as they were afore the making of this Act'.[41] It was therefore constantly cited after the Reformation, both in the printed literature and in court, by common lawyers as well as by civilians.[42] Many passages were incorporated into Gibson's *Codex*, and (perhaps chiefly through that medium) continued to influence ecclesiastical law down to the present: there are frequent citations in the nineteenth-century case law, and as late as 1947 the draft revision of canon law produced by the Archbishops' Commission contains numerous marginal references to Lyndwood.[43] According to Thomas Fuller, the book 'will be valued by the judicious

40 Cheney, 'Lyndwood's *Provinciale*', p. 177. It is not certain whether this direction was ever carried out. The autograph was last heard of in Oxford, in the possession of an executor, in 1448.

41 Submission of the Clergy 1534, 25 Hen. VIII, c. 19, s. 7. This proviso is still in force, though it was intended to be transitional until a revision of the canon law had been achieved. A committee of canonists chaired by Dr Richard Gwent, Dean of Arches, produced a draft outline code in 1535 which survives in the British Library (MS Add. 48040, fos 13r–104v), but it was not acceptable to the common lawyers and was abandoned. For the failure of Cranmer's 1552 commission, see below, p. 61 n. 18.

42 See, e.g., R. H. Helmholz, *Roman Canon Law in Reformation England* (Cambridge, 1990), pp. 68, 143, 145.

43 *The Canon Law of the Church of England: Being the Report of the Archbishops' Commission on Canon Law* (1947).

whilst learning and civility have a being'.44 But Fuller did not foresee a world in which Latin would no longer be taught in schools.

44 T. Fuller, *The Church-History of Britain* (1655), ii, p. 176.

Henry Swinburne B.C.L. († 1624)
Detail from his funeral monument in York Minster, photographed by the author.

By permission of the Dean of York

6

Henry Swinburne

HE first post-Reformation English canonist in our series seems, on the face of his *curriculum vitae*, a very different kind of lawyer from the medieval writers previously described. He was not a doctor of law, and seems to have spent only a short time at university. He went up to Oxford as a relatively mature student in 1576,[1] having already served an apprenticeship as clerk in the registrar's office at York and having become a notary public and actuary of the Consistory Court in the early 1570s. He was born and educated in the city of York, and came to the attention of the ecclesiastical authorities there as a promising clerk at about the age when more fortunate youngsters were sent to Oxford or Cambridge. Swinburne's course of study therefore began as a local boy employed in office work, and in the routines of clerical writing: a preparation which, as in other spheres of law also, could prove as valuable as college life for an active mind.

It is thought that the young clerk was taken under the wing of Dr Richard Percy, who was Commissary of the Exchequer Court at York from 1570. Swinburne later wrote of Percy with great deference, and reported in 1590 that he was engaged upon the preparation of a code of English canon law, 'now well towardes accomplishment'.[2] Percy at the least provided Swinburne with an exemplar, and it may

1 Probably in his early twenties.
2 Swinburne, *Testaments* (1591), sig. B2.

well be that he assisted more positively in arranging for the latter to spend three years at Oxford.3 At any rate, we know that Swinburne went up to Hart Hall in 1576 and studied law. The formal study of canon law had been ended at both universities forty years earlier, by order of Henry VIII's commissioners, and since then Oxford and Cambridge had possessed only unitary faculties of civil law. As a result, degrees in civil law were now the only recognised academical qualification for practising in the ecclesiastical courts,4 though it seems very likely that the instruction included frequent reference to canon law.5 Swinburne graduated as bachelor of civil law from Broadgates Hall (now Pembroke College) in 1579.6

Two years after graduation, Swinburne was admitted as one of the very small group of advocates practising in the ecclesiastical courts at York. Very little is known of these provincial bars, save that they were apparently independent of Canterbury. Although a matter of custom rather than of written law, it was in practice necessary to possess a doctorate in law before admission as an advocate in the Court of Arches,7 and it is these scarlet-robed advocates, mostly

---

3 The suggestion is made by R. A. Marchant, *The Church under the Law* (Cambridge, 1969), pp. 43, 45; and see J. D. M. Derrett, *Henry Swinburne, Civil Lawyer of York*, Borthwick Papers, 44 (York, 1973), p. 6. What follows is based very largely on Marchant and Derrett. See also the notice by A. F. Pollard in *DNB*, xix, pp. 228–29.

4 The present distinction between the title of Oxford doctors of law (D.C.L.) and that of their Cambridge counterparts (LL.D. – which is *doctor in jure*, in the oral form of admission) is of relatively recent origin. It will nevertheless be followed below, for convenience.

5 Helmholz, *Roman Canon Law in Reformation England* (Cambridge, 1990), p. 152.

6 A. Wood, *Athenae oxonienses* (1815 edn), ii, col. 289.

7 The only degree required by legislation was that of bachelor of canon or civil law, added in Archbishop Stratford's statutes (1342)

members of Doctors' Commons, whom we tend to think of as the English civilians. But there was no need for a northern practitioner to belong to the London society in Knightrider Street,[8] and there was no corresponding society in York. At York, moreover, a bachelor's degree in law was a sufficient qualification, and only a minority of the advocates had doctorates. Swinburne's son Toby was similarly admitted as an advocate at Durham without a doctor's degree.[9] Some northern advocates did trouble to acquire the same formal qualifications as their southern counterparts, perhaps in the hope of high office. In York Minster there is a demi-figure of Sir William Ingram LL.D. († 1623), Commissary of York, wearing a laced gown; he possessed a Cambridge doctorate in law, and was an advocate of the Arches, but was never admitted to Doctors' Commons.[10] But it seems that the main reason why Swinburne did not stay at Oxford to proceed to the doctorate was matrimonial. His marriage, while in residence, disqualified him from the fellowship which might have given him the necessary financial support. It became essential for him to earn a living at once.

Henry Swinburne practised as an advocate at York from 1581 until his death in 1624. Traces of his practice have survived in the form of some opinions, written in English,

---

to the 1295 requirement of at least four years' legal study and a year's attendance on the courts: *Concilia Magnae Britanniae*, ed. D. Wilkins (1737), ii, p. 688; P. Brand, *The Origins of the English Legal Profession* (Oxford, 1992), p. 149. Although Stratford's statute said 'doctor or bachelor', the requirement of a doctorate was universally observed by the sixteenth century and was said by Ayliffe and Burn to be a custom of England.

8 Doctors' Commons had moved in 1568 from Paternoster Row to Mountjoy House in Knightrider Street (rebuilt after the Great Fire); and it remained there until the premises were sold in 1865.

9 Marchant, *The Church under the Law*, p. 249 (in 1637). He proved to be a papist delinquent: Derrett, *Henry Swinburne*, p. 9.

10 Squibb, *Doctors' Commons*, p. 207.

which have been discovered in Durham.[11] Like all practising civilians, he concurrently held administrative and judicial offices, the chief of which were as Commissary of the Exchequer Court of York (1604–24) and Commissary of the Dean and Chapter of York (1613–24). The Exchequer Court was primarily concerned with testamentary business, and it seems a likely inference from the subject of Swinburne's first treatise that he had been involved in its affairs since Dr Percy's time. Quite apart from his experience in clerkship and in private practice, there was also judicial deputising: by this means Swinburne had, for instance, been holding deanery courts in the 1590s.[12]

Lowly though his background may have been, Swinburne's reputation places him in the ranks of the famous; and indeed his fame is deserved. He was the first writer on the canon law in English, and he adopted a felicitous informal style designed to be understood by laymen as well as experts. His principal work, *A Briefe Treatise of Testaments and Last Wills* (1590/91), was to pass through several editions and – like a modern textbook – evolve in the hands of successive editors during an active lifetime of some two centuries. His second work, *A Treatise of Spousals or Matrimonial Contracts* (1686), was published posthumously from an incomplete manuscript now in Lincoln's Inn.[13]

The Treatise Of Testaments

The greater of Swinburne's two treatises was printed by John Windet in 1590,[14] with the characteristically prolix

---

11 In Durham Cathedral, MS Raine 124. One of them is printed in Derrett, *Henry Swinburne*, p. 29.
12 Marchant, *The Church under the Law*, p. 120.
13 Lincoln's Inn, MS Misc. 577. Some unpublished portions also remain in manuscript.
14 The date on the title-page is 1590, but the colophon is dated 1591.

title, *A Briefe Treatise of Testaments and Last Willes, Very profitable to be understoode of all the Subjects of this Realme of England, (desirous to know,* Whether, Whereof, *and* How, *they may make their Testaments: and by what meanes the same may be* effected *or* hindered,*) and no lesse delightfull, aswell for the rarenes of the worke, as of the easines of the stile, and method: Compiled of such lawes Ecclesiasticall and Civill, as be not repugnant to the lawes, customes, or statutes of this Realme, nor derogatorie to the Prerogative Royall ... By the Industrie of Henrie Swinburn,*[15] *Bachelar of the Civill Lawe.* It was seen through the press by Swinburne himself, whose care is evident from the fact that copies of the first edition contain corrections on pasted slips, some even bearing further corrections in ink made at the author's direction.[16] The exception clause on the title-page was an allusion to the statute of 1534 under which, pending a projected review of the ecclesiastical law, the old canon law was to continue in force so far as it was not 'contrariant or repugnant to the King's prerogative royal or the customs, laws or statutes of this realm'.[17] Swinburne mentions in his preface the continuing failure to produce a new code,[18]

15 The name is spelled Swinburne at the end of the dedication and the preface, and this is the spelling usually preferred.

16 Derrett, *Henry Swinburne,* p. 11.

17 Submission of the Clergy 1534, 25 Hen. VIII, c. 19, s. 2; quoted above, p. 54; renewed by 27 Hen. VIII, c. 15; 35 Hen. VIII, c. 16.

18 A commission had finally been appointed in 1552, under the provisions of the statute 3 & 4 Edw. VI, c. 11: see *Acts of the Privy Council,* iii, pp. 382, 410, 471; *Calendar of Patent Rolls, 1550–53,* pp. 114 (preparatory sub-committee of eight), 354 (full commission of thirty-two). A draft code, revised by Archbishop Cranmer, was prepared, but it was defeated by the opposition of the Earl of Northumberland in 1553. The draft was published by John Foxe as *Reformatio legum* (1571; new edn by E. Cardwell, Oxford, 1850), but was never approved by Parliament or Convocation. Cf. *The Reformation of the Ecclesiastical Laws of England,* ed. J. C. Spalding (Kirksville, Missouri, 1992), which is the text of

although his patron Dr Percy had made good headway with a draft, and he feelingly indicates the reason:

> Great and wonderful is the number of the manifolde writers of the Civill and Ecclesiasticall Lawes, and so huge is the multitude of their sundrie sorts of books ... (apparent monuments of their endlesse and invincible labours) that in my conceite, it is impossible for any one man to read over the hundred part of their works, though living an hundred yeeres hee did intende none other worke.

The result of this failure was that the ecclesiastical law of England was 'secretly hidden from the subjects of this realme in corners of many bookes of straunge countries, and forreine language'. To remedy this, he had brought the subject into a 'narrow compasse' – a mere 600 pages – with the hope that 'this one litle booke may serve in steed of many great volumes'. He was apologetic about writing in English, but his object was to make the work as widely available as possible. Nevertheless, he hoped the book would also be of use to the 'Justinianists, or yong students of the Civill law', and for their special benefit he provided full references to authorities in the margin, in abbreviated Latin.

The nearest equivalent texts of the common law, the readings on the Statute of Wills 1540 by such as James Dyer (Middle Temple, 1552) and Ambrose Gilbert (Lincoln's Inn, 1556), consisted principally of lists of hypothetical cases connected by a few disjointed generalisations. By contrast, Swinburne's orderly exposition was a model of clarity and scientific technique. The scheme of the book was set out in an analytical table, reminiscent of the later schemes of Finch

---

a working draft (BL, MS Harley 426) rather than the final version: see the review by D. MacCulloch in *Journal of Ecclesiatical History*, 44 (1993), pp. 309–10.

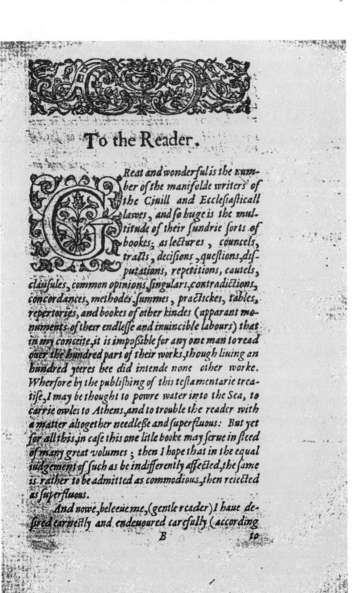

To the Reader.

Reat and wonderful is the number of the manifolde writers of the Ciuill and Ecclesiasticall lawes, and so huge is the multitude of their sundrie sorts of bookes; as lectures, councels, tracts, decisions, questions, disputations, repetitions, cautels, clausules, common opinions, singulars, contradictions, concordances, methodes summes, practickes, tables, repertories, and bookes of other kindes (apparant monuments of their endlesse and inuincible labours) that in my conceite, it is impossible for any one man to read ouer the hundred part of their works, though liuing an hundred yeeres hee did intende none other worke. Wherfore by the publishing of this testamentarie treatise, I may be thought to powre water into the Sea, to carrie owles to Athens, and to trouble the reader with a matter altogether needlesse and superfluous: But yet for all this, in case this one litle booke may serue in steed of many great volumes; then I hope that in the equal iudgement of such as be indifferently affected, the same is rather to be admitted as commodious, then reiected as superfluous.

And nowe, beleeue me, (gentle reader) I haue desired earnestly and endeuoured carefully (according

B   to

Swinburne on *Testaments*, showing the preface to the 1590 edition.

By permission of Cambridge University Library

and Hale, arranging and sub-dividing the whole subject in diagrammatic form. First, with due warnings about the danger of definitions, he defines testament, will, codicil and legacy. Then he considers capacity, subject-matter, form and interpretation, the appointment and duties of executors, and finally the factors which might vitiate a testament. The treatment is decidedly bookish, and it may be questioned – notwithstanding Swinburne's extensive practical experience – how far it squared with English practice. For instance, he treats heresy, apostasy, manifest usury, incest and sodomy as disqualifications from testatorship, although he concedes that English law departed from the general canon law in not recognising prodigality as a disqualification; yet for none of these propositions, though supported by an impressive array of continental learning, is any English authority or example cited.[19] Swinburne's discussion of the proof of insanity makes the important point that a witness could not depose merely that the deceased was mad, but must give evidence of the supporting facts. Yet his examples were derived from books: witnesses might say that 'they did see him throw stones against the windowes, or did see him usually to spit in men's faces, or being asked a question they did see him hisse like a goose or barke lyke a dogge'. These homely examples are derived not from experience of the Exchequer Court of York but from the writings of the continental jurists Baldus († 1400?), Corneus († 1492), Decius († 1536), Mascardi († 1588) and Mantica († 1614). Then again, in considering the evidence needed to prove bastardy, Swinburne relies on ancient authors as establishing that a woman could influence the appearance of her off-spring by the image in her mind at the time of conception,[20] and that men became barren at the age of eighty 'if not

19 Swinburne, *Testaments*, fos 54v–60v.
20 Ibid., fos 162r–164r.

before'.[21] In a partial concession to modern natural science, however, the author says that judges in deciding such questions might rely on what we call expert evidence – he treated it as advice – given by physicians, midwives, 'and especially such as bee skilfull in astrologie'.[22]

The book certainly achieved its object, and it represents a landmark in jurisprudence. It made available to the lay public and their advisers – including, ultimately, a legally trained posterity unable to cope with the original sources – the essential gist of masses of obscure Latin texts, summarising in many cases the arguments on both sides of a question. As a result, Swinburne remained the first recourse on the subject for over two hundred years. The treatise was reprinted by the Company of Stationers (who in 1607 acquired the copyright) in 1611, 1635 and 1640. The 1611 edition was published, of course, in Swinburne's lifetime, and it claimed on the title-page to have been 'newly corrected and augmented with sundry principall additions, by the industrie of Henry Swinburn'. The following two editions seem to have been treated as one by the trade, for the 'very much enlarged' version which appeared in 1677, under the imprint of the law printers George Sawbridge, Thomas Roycroft and William Rawlins, was described as the fourth edition. The price of this new edition was 7s.[23] Further editions were produced, and sold at the price of one guinea, in 1728 and 1743. A Dublin edition appeared in 1793, in two octavo volumes, described as the seventh edition. The

21 Ibid., fo. 164v. In the case of aged men, the antique learning was not that they were unable to perform sexual acts but that they could not thereby procreate: idem, *Spousals*, p. 50.
22 Ibid., fo. 166r.
23 E. Arber, ed., *The Term Catalogues, 1668–1709*, i (1903), p. 286. The second-hand price of the older editions had been quoted in the 1670s as 10s.: *The General Catalogue of Books Printed in England ... Collected by Robert Clavell* (1675), p. 62.

English seventh (and final) edition was heavily edited by the conveyancer John Joseph Powell († 1801) of the Middle Temple, prepared for the press by James Wake of Lincoln's Inn, and published in three volumes by William Clarke and Sons in 1803. It is clear proof of the continuing importance of Swinburne's text to all English lawyers, and of its accessibility, that this final edition should have been the work of barristers trained in the law of real property rather than of a civilian from Doctors' Commons.

The Treatise *Of Spousals*

Swinburne's second treatise was never finished, and the completed portion was not printed in his own lifetime. There is some evidence that he intended it as the first part of a larger work on matrimony, with two further books on marriage and divorce.[24] The finished part was printed posthumously in 1686, at the hand of an anonymous editor, by Samuel Roycroft, on behalf of Robert Clavell, at the Peacock in St Paul's Churchyard. It is much shorter than *Testaments*, occupying only 240 pages exclusive of the preliminaries.

By 'spousals' (*sponsalia*), Swinburne meant the contract to marry, whether by words of the present or future tense, and he set out a great deal of rather esoteric erudition on the construction and effect of various kinds of engagement. Despite the heavy use of pedantic scholarship in the continental tradition, the lightness of touch found in *Testaments* is even more evident here. Swinburne wrote as we may suppose he spoke – 'here methinks some man doth pull me by the sleeve, and tell me in my ear, that this distinction fighteth with the former definition' – 'yet is not the second

---

24 The editor of the 1686 edition says that Swinburne left unfinished notes on these portions. Swinburne, *Spousals* itself contains forward references to the unfinished part.

part [of an opinion] able to withstand the Canon shot ...
but must needs also fall and be battered with the same
Bullet'.25 More rigorous editing of such passages might have
reduced the length of the book, but would have detracted
from its charm.

As one might expect from an ageing ecclesiastical judge,
the author's opinions on personal behaviour lean towards
the conservative side. In his discussion of whether a contract
to marry made by infants could be ratified at full age by
conduct short of cohabitation or copulation, he argues that
kissing and embracing could be regarded as implied ratifi-
cation. Some, he concedes, argue that such evidence is
inconclusive, 'because these amorous actions ... are often
practised as preambles and allurement rather to accomplish
the accomplishment of unlawful lusts, and to quench the
flames of youthful desires, than to tye the indissoluble knot
of chast wedlock'. But Swinburne thought this an unchari-
table supposition, because one should not presume the worst
of people (*delictum non praesumitur*).26 Elsewhere he allows
that people might marry once they were past the age of
childbearing, for mutual solace: 'But I speak this rather to
defend the marriage of the aged from unlawfulness, than to
commend it for comliness.'27 His lack of sympathy with the
times positively boils over when it comes to the subject of
rings, where he inveighs against 'the Vanity, Lasciviousness,
and intollerable Pride of these our days, wherein every skip-
ping Jack, and every flirting Jill, must not only be ring'd
(forsooth) very daintily, but must have some special Jewel
or Favour besides, as though they were descended of
some noble house ...'28 Here we find a mature Swinburne

25 Ibid., pp. 8, 205. The words here omitted show that 'Canon shot'
   was meant as appalling pun.
26 Ibid., p. 42.
27 Ibid., p. 50.
28 Ibid., p. 209.

venturing to be himself, in contrast with the objective but detached and seemingly unworldly compiler of learned texts. In either character, Swinburne is still pleasing to read and easy to understand.

For all its lively appeal, this second work was not destined to enjoy the same success as *Testaments*, because the subject-matter was already archaic by the time it was printed. Had Swinburne finished the remainder of the projected volume, with the sections on marriage and divorce, it would doubtless have outshone *Testaments*, and might have lasted even until the present day. In the event, there was only one further edition, in 1711.

Swinburne's Achievement

Swinburne's failure to take the doctorate, as we have noted, had more to do with his personal circumstances than his prowess in the Oxford law school. Certainly his writings demonstrate that a doctor's degree was not an absolute prerequisite of legal learning in the Latin tradition. Though he wore his learning lightly, with touches of humour and homespun philosophy, his scholarly pains are evident in the copious citations, which have been carefully analysed by Professor Derrett. Over 225 authors are cited, ranging from the classics to the latest continental writers on canon law. Swinburne was not only familiar with the modern English reporters, Dyer and Plowden, and naturally with the *Decisiones rotae*, but more remarkably he was also au fait with the law reports of the *ius commune*: with d'Afflitto and Capece of Naples, with Corsier of Toulouse, and with Boyer of Bordeaux. The enormous range of learning which he displayed naturally raises the question where Swinburne could have read so many books. It seems unlikely that he can have owned them all himself. Professor Derrett made the suggestion that he must have paid regular visits to Doctors'

Commons; but it now seems unlikely that there was any library there during his lifetime.[29] More likely the source was the cathedral library at York, together with any private libraries to which Swinburne gained access, augmented by such study notes as he had brought back from Oxford. If only half of these law books were available in York, that city can have been no mean research centre in canon law in the time of James I. Visitors to York Minster may still see Swinburne's kneeling effigy habited in a black laced gown, presumably of his baccalaureate, but without a hood (p. 56 above);[30] if this represents his Oxford academical dress, he may nevertheless be hailed as a professor of the informal law school at York.

Provincial in his background and occupations, Swinburne was certainly not provincial in his thought and writing. Professor Helmholz has recently demonstrated the continued vitality of continental jurisprudence in England after the Reformation:[31] it was no objection in an Elizabethan ecclesiastical court that a living foreign author was an arrant papist. But the cosmopolitan character of canon law was not to continue much longer. Swinburne was one of the last major English legal writers in the European *ius commune* tradition, if not the last. His bold decision to write in plain English carried much of that learning effortlessly into the nineteenth century; but freedom of access to that scholarship

29 G. D. Squibb, *Doctors' Commons* (Oxford, 1977), p. 88, questioning Derrett, *Henry Swinburne*, pp. 18, 32.
30 The gown is worn over a flower-figured cassock buttoned down the front; he also wears a starched ruff, and a black skull cap. The arms displayed below the effigy are: *Per fess gules and argent three cinquefoils counterchanged* (Swinburne), impaling, *Sable a chevron between three leopards' faces or, a crescent gules for difference* (?Wentworth).
31 R. H. Helmholz, *Roman Canon Law in Reformation England* (Cambridge, 1990).

began to disappear with his generation. The heavy, leather-bound 'monuments of endlesse and invincible labours' were about to enjoy a long retirement.

7

Francis Clarke

 T could surely give no great offence to the departed doctors of the Arches if a series devoted to famous canon lawyers were to include a passing tribute to a few members of the lower branch of the profession, the proctors. It is true that they have not received as much national recognition as their precursors in the series; of the two we have selected, Clarke earned but a few anonymous lines in the *Dictionary of National Biography*, Oughton none at all.[1] Even their dates of death have eluded discovery. Yet among ecclesiastical lawyers they have a lasting place of honour as the principal writers on the procedure of the church courts in England in its developed form. As Clarke pointed out in the preface to his book, addressed to the law students at Oxford and Cambridge, the university law faculties were wont to teach the substance but to overlook the practice. Law graduates intending to earn a living from their subject therefore had to start virtually from the beginning. No doubt the age-old method of acquiring a mastery of the procedural forms, as in the common-law courts, was to serve as clerk in an office and copy out precedents. There are plenty of surviving collections of precedents of forms used in ecclesiastical litigation and administration to bear witness to this method

---

1 Oughton did, however, achieve a brief entry (by P. G. Stein) in the *Biographical Dictionary of the Common Law*, ed. A. W. B. Simpson (1984), p. 394, something which Clarke failed to attain. For Oughton, see below, p. 89.

of information. Yet until the end of the sixteenth century there were no written guides to procedure or to the oral forms used in court. There is some evidence that Dr John Hammond († 1589) prepared an outline guide, called a *Brief for Judiciary Practice*;[2] but this does not seem to have circulated widely or to have been very substantial. It is hardly surprising, therefore, that when Francis Clarke produced his full-length treatise in the 1590s it soon gained a wide circulation, albeit in manuscript.

Francis Clarke (or Clerke) remains an obscure personage, despite recent efforts to find out more about him.[3] He may have been related to Bartholomew Clerke († 1590), Dean of Arches, but this is no more than a guess.[4] Without attending university, or at any rate without staying to take a degree, he went straight into practice in the 1550s and was admitted a Proctor of the Arches in 1564. He acted for the University of Oxford, and in 1594 received from that university the degree of bachelor of civil law by special grace. In his supplication for the degree, Clarke stated that he wished to be able to adorn his name on the title-page of a book which he

2 There are two late copies in Cambridge University Archives: MS Collect. Admin. 30(2) (prefaced to a copy of Clarke); MS Collect. Admin. 35(2): see J. H. Baker, *Catalogue of English Legal MSS in Cambridge University Library* (Woodbridge, 1996), pp. 663–64, 667. Dr Hammond was admitted as an advocate in the Court of Arches in 1569: Squibb, *Doctors' Commons*, p. 157. For some similar but anonymous tracts, see Helmholz, *Roman Canon Law in Reformation England*, pp. 131–33.

3 The principal study is by Professor J. D. M. Derrett, 'The Works of Francis Clerke, Proctor', *Studia et documenta historiae et iuris*, 40 (1974), pp. 52–66. Most of the information given below is derived from Professor Derrett's helpful paper.

4 Professor Derrett conjectures that they were brothers. But Francis would have to have been an elder brother, which would have been odd. Dr Clerke's father was a Somerset notary. There were two other advocates called Clerke at this period, both Cambridge doctors of law.

A proctor, writing at a table, and apparently receiving clients.
Woodcut from a pamphlet on the abuses of the spiritual courts,
1641.

had just written. This is evidently the treatise on practice in
the ecclesiastical courts, although in most versions (including
that printed in 1666) the preface is dated 1596. The treatise
begins with a discussion of judges and jurisdictions; it next
deals with process (citations and excommunication), plead-
ing (from libel to litiscontestatio), proofs, and sentence; then
with summary causes and appeals; and, finally, with specific
subjects such as marriage, divorce, tithes, defamation, patronage, dilapidations and wills (including inventories and
accounts). Clarke wrote a companion treatise on the practice
of the Court of Admiralty, in which he also worked as a
proctor, and this (for want of any serious competitor) enjoyed
an even longer life than its ecclesiastical counterpart.5

5 F. Clarke, *Praxis curiae admiralitatis Angliae* (1st edn, 1667). Re-
printed in 1679, 1722, 1743, and 1829. An English translation by
J. E. Hall was included in his *Law and Practice of the Admiralty*
(Baltimore, Maryland, 1809).

It is evident from the preface, as well as from the Oxford
supplicat, that Clarke intended the work to be published for
the use of students. What is not known is whether he sought
to have it printed. It was not, in fact, printed in his lifetime,
but it was nevertheless effectively published in manuscript.
Books of the common law were widely circulated in manuscript at this time, and since the users of Clarke would not
have been numerous it may have been felt that printing was
too uncertain a venture. On the other hand, copying by the
student may have been thought to possess some educational
value. Whatever the original plan, manuscripts of the book
on the church courts were made in large numbers. Over fifty
survive, many of them in diocesan registries,[6] and they bear
a number of differing titles. The commonest is *De curiis
ecclesiasticis quae celebrantur auctoritate reverendi patris
Cantuariensis archiepiscopi infra civitatem Londoniensem,*[7]
but we also find, for instance, *Praxis causarum Curiae de
Arcubus;*[8] *Practica celeberrima ac quotidiana observata et
usitata in curiis reverendissimi Cantuarensis archiepiscopi;*[9]
or the more generalised *Practica clericorum seu adol-
escentium ad scienciam via de causis et curiis ecclesiasticis,*[10]
and *Procuratorium ac modus postulandi in causis et curiis
ecclesiasticis.*[11] There are some signs of successive recen-
sions in the manuscripts, most notably in the list of judges
and officials in tit. 2, which was updated several times
down to the mid 1620s, but also in a number of additions

---

6 Helmholz adds over thirty manuscripts to Derrett's list: *Roman
    Canon Law in Reformation England,* pp. 128–29, 196–97.
7 CUL, MSS Dd. 2.31, Hh. 3.12, Mm. 4.30 and Add. 4469; Cam-
    bridge University Archives, MSS Collect. Admin. 30(6), 31 and
    32; Harvard Law School, MSS 1050, 1214.
8 Catholic University of America, Washington, D.C., MS 180.
9 H. E. Huntington Library, San Marino, California, MS HM
    35072.
10 Harvard Law School, MS 1037.
11 CUL, MS Add. 4469, fo. iv (separate title-page).

and emendations. Copies were still being taken in the 1660s.[12] Some manuscripts have marginal references to authorities, including contemporary works by continental authors, and it may be that these were added by successive owners.[13] Through constant copying, however, many of the texts became quite corrupt.

It was, alas, a corrupt text which was put into print. The edition appeared in 1666, in Dublin, under the editorship of Thomas Bladen D.D. († 1686), Dean of Ardfert. The title of this edition is: *Praxis Francisci Clarke, tam ius dicentibus quam aliis omnibus qui in foro ecclesiastico versantur apprimè utilis.*[14] The editor was not a lawyer, and he seems to have taken little trouble to make sense of the text by comparing manuscripts or correcting obvious blunders. Nor was any scholarly apparatus included. The edition was dedicated to James Margetson, Archbishop of Armagh, Primate of All Ireland, and Michael Boyle, Archbishop of Dublin, Primate and Lord Chancellor of Ireland, but the editor's purpose in producing it is not apparent. It was reprinted in 1684 in London, but, although the title-page claimed that it had been much corrected, this was essentially the same corrupt text. No further printing was undertaken, and no modern scholar has accepted Professor Derrett's challenge to produce a satisfactory edition. The reason for the eclipse of Clarke's treatise was twofold: it was overtaken firstly by a more accessible work for beginners, and then by a far superior work for practitioners.

The latter must be deferred until we reach the eighteenth century.[15] The book for beginners was Henry Consett's *The*

---

12 E.g. Harvard Law School, MS 1037 (copy dated 1666).

13 See Helmholz, *Roman Canon Law in Reformation England*, pp. 129–31.

14 The printer was Nathaniel Thompson, for the bookseller John Leach of Castle Street.

15 Below, p. 89 (Oughton's *Ordo judiciorum*).

Practice of the Spiritual or Ecclesiastical Courts (1685), to
which was added (pp. 401–8) 'A Brief Discourse of the Struc-
ture and Manner of Forming the Declaration'. This guide
was written in English and, without being a word by word
translation, it was heavily based on Clarke and in many
places exactly the same. Indeed, Consett acknowledged in
his preface his own 'small experience ... in these concerns',
and hoped the reader would not 'quarrel that I use Mr
Clarke's words'. Here, then, was something approaching a
vernacular edition of Clarke, with some references added;
and it proved sufficiently useful for it to be reprinted three
times (in 1685, 1700 and 1708). Nothing is known of Consett,
who would seem from the tone of his preface not to have
been a practitioner.[16]

---

16 Cf. W. S. Holdsworth, *History of English Law*, xii (1938), p. 617,
who points out that Consett dates the preface from York and
suggests that he practised in the northern province. Consett does
not not appear to have been a university graduate or a barrister.

8

John Godolphin

HE cessation of formal instruction in canon law at the time of the Reformation, and the consequent slow decline in general familiarity with the older Latin sources, brought a corresponding need for English ecclesiastical law to be systematised in a form which could be comprehended by members of the clergy and others – including common lawyers – whose professions brought them into contact with it. It is noticeable that the advocates of Doctors' Commons did not play a major part in supplying that need. The common lawyers had begun to make a contribution, especially in areas which straddled the lay and spiritual jurisdictions, though their handbooks for parsons do not really deserve to be regarded as legal classics.[1] Their best contributions to learning in the ecclesiastical sphere were in the inns of court readings on benefices, a subject which had always been within the

---

1 E. g. W. Hughes, *Parson's Law* (1641); W. Sheppard, *Parson's Guide* (1654); S. Degge, *The Parson's Counsellor* (1676; 7th edn, 1820); G. Meriton, *The Parson's Monitor* (1681); W. Nelson, *The Rights of the Clergy* (1709); W. Bohun, *The Law of Tithes* (1730). These are principally about tithes. W. Watson, *Clergyman's Law* (1701), though published under the name of a real clergyman (who had taken the LL.D. but went into the church instead), is said to have been written by a barrister of Gray's Inn called Place: see 1 Bl. Comm. 391n. A Henry Place was called in 1685, an Edward Place in 1690: *The Pension Book of Gray's Inn*, ed. R. J. Fletcher, ii (1910), pp. 82, 110.

province of the common law.[2] First and foremost among
the unprinted readings on benefices was that delivered in
the Middle Temple in 1619 by James Whitelocke, B. C. L.,
subsequently a King's Bench judge, who had the unusual
distinction for a common lawyer of having taken some legal
education at Oxford.[3] However, the civilians had a further
contribution to make before non-lawyers conquered the field
in the eighteenth century. In parallel with common lawyers
such as Serjeants Rolle and Sheppard, they brought in what
might be called the 'abridgment phase' of English canon
law. And, in the process, they began the process of assimilation with the common law of the secular courts.

  John Godolphin (1617–78) was descended from the ancient
Cornish family of that name, being the third son of John
Godolphin of Budock, though he was born in the Isles of Scilly
when his father was serving there.[4] He read law at Gloucester
Hall, Oxford, fated to become in the next century the only
college at Oxford or Cambridge ever to be dissolved by the
death of all its members.[5] He took his doctorate of civil law
in 1643, but it is unlikely that he became a practising advocate
at that troubled period, and his name does not appear in the
register of Doctors' Commons until 1655. Unlike the majority
of civilians on the eve of civil war, who allied themselves

---

2 An advowson was a species of real property recoverable in the
  royal courts by writ of right of advowson or quare impedit. A
  reading on advowsons by John Dodderidge (Middle Temple,
  1603) was printed as *A Compleat Parson* (1630).
3 At least eighteen manuscripts are known. Comparable in its display of erudition was Francis's Tate's reading (Middle Temple,
  1607) on tithes, which survives in a unique, possibly autograph,
  text: CUL, MS Oo. 6.92(1) (anonymous, but identifiable with
  some confidence as Tate's).
4 There is a brief unsigned biography in *DNB*, viii, p. 41. There is
  an annotated pedigree of the family in S. G. March, *The Godol-
  phins* (1930). Dr Godolphin resided for a time in Cornwall but
  settled in Clerkenwell and was buried there.
5 It was refounded as Worcester College.

with the royalist cause and the Laudian church, Godolphin was a fervent Puritan, and he first burst into print as a religious writer shortly after the execution of Charles I. His *Holy Limbec* (1650) purported to be a distillation of the spirit from the letter of the Scriptures, and it was followed by another metaphorical title, *The Holy Arbor* (1651), whose contents were 'collected from many orthodox laborers in the Lord's vineyard'. In 1653, still in his thirties, he obtained the appointment of Judge of the Admiralty, and it was in recognition of this important post – especially important to the civilian world after the abolition of episcopal jurisdiction under Cromwell – that he was in 1655 admitted to Doctors' Commons and forthwith elected president of that society.[6] His judgeship was, of course, declared void at the Restoration, though he is said to have received some legal office from the King in compensation.[7] He seems then to have entered private practice as a civilian advocate, presumably in the church courts as well as in Admiralty. Godolphin was obviously a considerable scholar and bibliophile. The sale catalogue of his library shows that, besides a large general collection, he possessed over 350 volumes of canon or civil law, including pamphlets and manuscripts (with two versions of Clarke's *Praxis*), and nearly 200 volumes of English law.[8]

In the Restoration year he published his *View of the*

6 Squibb, *Doctors' Commons*, p. 177.

7 According to *DNB* and Squibb he became King's Advocate; but he does not appear in the list of King's Advocates-General in J. Sainty, *A List of English Law Officers*, Selden Society, Supplementary Series, 7 (1987), p. 77. Perhaps he was King's Advocate in Admiralty Causes.

8 *Catalogus variorum et insignium librorum . . . D. Johannis Godolphin, J.U.D., et D. Oweni Phillips, A.M*, sold by William Cooper on 11 November 1678 (copy in CUL, Fff. 79[II]). It is assumed that the law books were all Godolphin's, but there is no way of separating the remaining lots. The count includes thirty-eight legal tracts listed on p. 36.

Admiral Jurisdiction, essentially a polemical defence of the jurisdiction against enroachments from the common law, but which has recently been given modified acclaim as 'the first attempt in published, literary form to state the case for the Admiralty jurisdiction'.[9] Our reason for including him among our famous canon lawyers is that in the 1670s he wrote two well-known abridgments of canon law. The first was *The Orphan's Legacy, or A Testamentary Abridgement* (1674; reprinted 1677, 1681, 1701), dealing with the law of testate and intestate succession, followed by his *Repertorium canonicum* (1678; reprinted 1680, 1687), covering the remainder of the canon law.

The former of these works received its imprimatur from Lord Shaftesbury, the Lord Chancellor, on 26 April 1673. According to its title-page, the subject was treated of 'as well according to the Common and Temporal, as Ecclesiastical and Civil Laws of this Realm'. In paying tribute to Swinburne, the author pointed out that, 'having been pleas'd to confine himself to the incomparable Lawes of his own Profession, [he] hath left the fairer Latitude for Variation, admitting him to have transcended all possibilities of Imitation'. On the very first page, Justinian jostles with Plowden and Brooke, and the author continuously fulfils his promise to provide a comprehensive treatment from the standpoint of both systems of law. There are three sections. The first, 'Of Last Wills and Testaments', is the shortest (forty-six pages), and deals with capacity and form in much the same manner as Swinburne, but with greater attention to the common law. Godolphin renders the scholastic Latin of the canonists in a homely manner, reminiscent of the avowedly

9 M. J. Prichard and D. E. C. Yale, *Hale and Fleetwood on Admiralty Jurisdiction*, Selden Society, 108 (1993), p. cxiii. See also D. Coquillette, *The Civilian Writers of Doctors' Commons, London* (Berlin, 1988), pp. 186–89. *DNB* also records a treatise by Godolphin on *Laws of the Admiralty*, not published until 1746.

Godolphin's *Abridgment of the Ecclesiastical Laws*, showing the title-page of the 1678 edition.

From a book in the possession of the author

inimitable Swinburne, as when he points out (citing Vas-
quez) that drunkenness does not invalidate a testament if
the mind is merely clouded or obscured by drink; the testator
must be, 'according to the Flaggon-phrase, as it were dead-
drunk' (p. 13). The second and much longer section (134
pages) is 'Of Executors and Administrators', and draws
heavily on common-law materials. In the final and longest
section (250 pages), 'Of Legacies and Devises', there is more
emphasis on the canon law, ending (ch. 26) with a distillation
of rules from the later canonical authors.

The full title of the larger work is *Repertorium canonicum:
or An Abridgment of the Ecclesiastical Laws of this Realm,
Consistent with the Temporal*, though the imprimaturs
(from Chief Justice North and the Bishop of London)
referred to it solely under its English title of *An Abridgment
of the Ecclesiastical Laws*. The book begins with a lengthy
introduction, in eighty-eight pages, surveying the history of
the church and ecclesiastical jurisdiction in England since
the time of the Anglo-Saxons and before,[10] in the same order
as the abridgment. Godolphin makes every effort to dispel
any lurking doubts about his political and religious sympathies. The royal supremacy, he declares on the first page,
is so fundamental that without it 'all that follows would be
but insignificant and disfigured cyphers'; the authority of
bishops and clergy is defended, even with approving reference to the Council of Trent; and an allusion is made to the
'late unnatural war in this kingdom' as a cause of the deso-
lation of many churches (p. 26). The abridgment itself
consists of forty-four non-alphabetical titles, filling 653
pages. The first thirteen titles concern office-holders in the
church, from the Supreme Governor (ch. 1) down to the

---

10 E.g., J. Godolphin, *Repertorium canonicum* (1678), pp. 24–25,
   where he discusses speculations that St Paul's was built on the
   site of a Roman temple of Diana and Westminster Abbey on the
   site of the temple of Apollo.

'sidemen' (ch. 13),[11] and including *en passant* forty pages
on the church courts and their jurisdiction (ch. 11). Chancellors, we learn, must be knowledgeable in the civil and
canon law, and for this reason a reverend Chancellor of
Gloucester, being a divine but not a law graduate, was
lawfully deprived by the High Commission in the time of
Charles I.[12] However, the degree of bachelor of civil law
will suffice – at any rate for a commissary – as was ruled
on demurrer in the 1590s.[13] The archdeacon (ch. 8) has an
ecclesiastical dignity and 'by the Canon law' a jurisdiction
'of a far larger extent than is now practicable with us'; also
'by the Canon law' he must be at least twenty-five years old
and a licentiate in law or divinity. It seems that, here and
elsewhere, 'the Canon law' is not necessarily to be equated
with current English ecclesiastical law. Godolphin merely
sets out the authorities, often without indicating whether,
how or when a particular rule ceased to bind in England.
He does, however, as in *The Testamentary Abridgement*,

11 Ibid., p. 167; he asserts that the churchwardens may not dispose
   of goods in their custody without the assent of 'the sidemen or
   vestry', and that 'the parishioners are a corporation to dispose of
   such personal things as appertain to the Church'. He derives the
   word sidemen from 'Synods-men' (ibid., p. 163).
12 *Dr Sutton's Case* (1626) Litt. Rep. 2, 22; Cro. Car. 65 (prohibition
   denied by the Common Pleas). Litt. Rep. 2 says he was deprived
   'pur ceo que il ne fuit Batchelor ou Doctor del Civil Ley de officio'.
   In 1627, Dr Sutton applied to the King's Bench for a prohibition,
   but with the same result: Noy 91; Latch 228; Godb. 390; Wm
   Jones 393. The judges in the second case included Dodderidge
   and Whitelocke JJ. (mentioned above).
13 *Pratt* v. *Stocke* (1594), cited as Hil. 35 Eliz., rot. 181; reported in
   Poph. 37 (cited as Mich. 33 & 34 Eliz., rot. 181); Cro. Eliz. 315
   (plaintiff counts on administration by Thomas Tayler LL.B.,
   Commissary to the Bishop of London; defendant pleads 37 Hen.
   VIII, c. 17; plaintiff demurs). The case was followed by the King's
   Bench in *Walker* v. *Lamb* (1632) Wm Jones 263; Cro. Car. 258
   (William Walker LL.B. appointed Official of the Archdeacon of
   Leicester and Commissary of the Bishop of Lincoln).

bring together the common law and the Latin authors. Indeed, there are far more common-law cases (from the year books down to the seventeenth century) than canonical texts. The common-law influence is especially dominant in his next nineteen chapters (chs 14–32), dealing with benefices and incumbents, advowsons and tithes. The last twelve chapters (chs 33–44) deal with miscellaneous matters within the ecclesiastical jurisdiction, including banns, adultery, bastardy, divorce, defamation, sacrilege, simony, blasphemy and heresy, councils and synods, and excommuniation. There is an obvious omission in that the abridgment contains no extended discussion of wills or intestate succession; but that is because *The Testamentary Abridgement* was evidently intended to serve as a companion volume.

The treatment veers, according to subject-matter, from the practical to the speculative. The chapter on tithes (ch. 32) is highly practical and includes an eighty-page abridgment-within-an-abridgment, in the form of an alphabetical list of subjects related to tithing, from *Abby-lands* to *Wool*, including such unusual legal sub-headings as *Bricks*, *Turkeys* and *Vetches* (none of which were tithable). Godolphin's treatment of adultery is less practically focused and ranges widely over the severe punishments inflicted in other laws. The author criticises the opinion, allegedly held by some in the Church of Rome, that it is 'far more repugnant to the Law of Nature that one woman should be joyned to two men than *e contra*' (p. 475): 'the feminine sex', he predicts, 'will give them but little thanks for this opinion'. Divorce is taken already to bear the primary meaning of dissolution of marriage, though of course in earlier texts (as Godolphin points out) it more often means nullity. The 'Civil and Canon Law do allow of divorce after a long absence', but this opinion is denied; again, we apparently see a distinction between 'Canon law' and current English law. Godolphin discusses at length the lawfulness of remarriage after divorce, which is treated as a matter of considerable controversy, since the Bible appears to countenance divorce *a vinculo* for adultery. The defamation jurisdiction was severely limited by the requirement that the accusation be of a spiritual rather than a temporal wrong. This rule would let in an accusation of being a witch's son, since this might be a reason for refusing ordination (p. 524), but not one of a common-law offence. However, the author reveals no regrets at the decline of this jurisdiction. In the preface (p. 63), he observes that, 'such ill-scented suits do savour worse being kept alive in a tribunal than they would by being buried in oblivion, especially if the defamed considered, that to forget injuries is the best use we can make of a bad memory'. The chapters on sacrilege and heresy are more historical than practical, and in the latter there is another alphabetical sub-abridgment (pp. 565–80) containing a curious list of heresies from *Acatiani* to *Vigilantinus*, followed by some non-Christian heresies (including, for the sake of absolute completeness, frog-worshipping). The conclusion (p. 583) is that 'the Prince of Darkness and the father of lyes hath in all ages, nations and Churches, his emissaries to infect them with heretical and blasphemous errors, but the gates or power of Hell to this day never could, nor to eternity ever shall prevail against the Truth'. The chapter on councils and synods includes a calendar of councils, based on Prideaux. The final two chapters are perhaps afterthoughts: chapter 43 contains notes on the medieval statutes concerning ecclesiastical jurisdiction; and the last treats of various common-law writs concerning benefices.

Godolphin's pair of abridgments represent the first substantial attempt to merge the canonical authorities with those of the common law, and thereby provide a comprehensive survey of all the rules of law relating to the church and its affairs in England. They share the general defect of all abridgments, in that the matter is not fully organised beyond the headings; and in his case they do not even have the benefit of the alphabet as a means of overall arrangement. They are, nevertheless, superior to the older common-law abridgments both in terms of the range of contents and the quality of exposition, and still offer a valuable short-cut for finding the ecclesiastical law of the seventeenth century. Moreover, they deserve much of the credit for the later systematic works which have built upon their foundation.

John Bettesworth LL.D. (1688–1751), President of Doctors' Commons 1710–51, showing the scarlet and miniver Cambridge congregation habit as worn by advocates in the Court of Arches (see p. 90). The sleeveless cope is derived from that seen on Lyndwood's brass (p. 45).

From a painting in private possession

9

John Ayliffe

ETWEEN Godolphin and Oughton we should
notice the sad figure of Dr John Ayliffe (1676–
1732), sometime Fellow of New College,
Oxford.[1] After reading law, taking his doctorate
of civil law in 1710, Ayliffe based himself in Oxford rather
than Doctors' Commons, and transacted some business as
proctor in the university court.[2] A passionate Whig, he seems
to have been a man of strong religious opinions and unwilling to keep quiet about matters which offended him. In what
purported to be a history of Oxford University, which he
published in 1714, he took the opportunity to criticise the
Clarendon Press and successive vice-chancellors for misap-
propriation of funds, and his own college for allowing its
reputation to decline as a result of internal quarrels, compounded by the 'supine negligence' of 'a late warden'. There
was not much enthusiasm for such robust freedom of expression in the Oxford of 1714, and Ayliffe paid a heavy
price when he was deprived of his degrees and driven out
of his fellowship – which he chose to resign rather than
withdraw his criticisms. Whether Ayliffe was right on these
questions is a matter for historians of Oxford University to
determine. He is, however, less controversially remembered
by posterity for his book, *Parergon juris canonici anglicani:
or a Commentary, by Way of Supplement to the Canons*

---

1 *DNB*, i, pp. 751–53 (biography by G. P. Macdonell).
2 Not proctor of the university.

and Constitutions of the Church of England, which was printed in large folio in 1726 (second edition, 1734).3 This was an alphabetical compendium of English canon law, with a historical preface, which he wrote for his own use as a practitioner and in the hope of some preferment. In the tradition of Lyndwood and Swinburne, Ayliffe allows his personality free rein in places, especially in his prolonged attack (pp. 231–33) on excessive drinking by the clergy. The book is written in a rather ornate style of English, and suffers from a failure to analyse or draw conclusions from the heaps of material which are piled into each heading. Viewed simply as a mine of information it is useful, especially since the compiler used authorities ranging from Justinian and classical authors down to recent reported decisions of the English courts, though it has to be admitted that a good deal of the material was derived directly from Godolphin.

3 He also wrote on ancient Roman law. In the year of his death (1732) was published his *The Law of Pledges, or Pawns, as it was in Use among the Romans*. Ayliffe was also the author of an uncompleted *New Pandect of Roman Civil Law*, published in 1734, two years after his death: as to which, see Coquillette, *Civilian Writers*, pp. 209–14. Professor Coquillette praises the latter (ibid., p. 212) as 'a formidable treasure house of scholarship'.

10

Thomas Oughton

N the eighteenth century the practising advocates all but surrendered the literature of English ecclesiastical law to others. But before it passed into the hands of non-lawyers, the literature of practice was considerably improved by the proctor Thomas Oughton († c. 1740). Oughton is as obscure personally as Francis Clarke, in whose tradition he followed, though Professor Stein has made the persuasive suggestion that he was the son of another Thomas Oughton, Registrar of the Court of Delegates. The younger Oughton was a deputy registrar of the same court until about 1720, but remained on the list of proctors until around 1740.[1] In 1713 he completed a manuscript entitled *Processus judiciarius*, which he handed over to a printer; but the entire stock (and also, it seems, the copy) was destroyed by fire.[2] With an enviable display of self-composure and determination, Oughton set about to rewrite the lost book, a task which occupied a further fifteen years. It finally appeared in 1728, in two volumes, as *Ordo judiciorum; sive methodus procedendi in negotiis et litibus in foro ecclesiastico-civili britannico et hibernico*.[3] It was

---

1 *Biographical Dictionary of the Common Law*, ed. A. W. B. Simpson (1984), p. 394 (note by P. G. Stein); lists of proctors in Chamberlayne's *Ancient State*.
2 Preface to the 1728 edn. The date is not given, but may be precisely calculated from the list of judges who subscribed.
3 The printer was J. Hooke at the sign of the Golden Rainbow ('ad Insigne Auratae-Iridis') in Fleet Street.

reprinted in 1738. According to Oughton, he took his new title from a book by a sixteenth-century Italian procedural writer, Roberto Maranta.4

Oughton's work, having been seen through the press by its author, is a far more elegant and accurate account of the subject than the garbled remains of Clarke. Dedicated to the judges and advocates of Doctors' Commons, it begins with a detailed account of the civilian profession and its customs, including the various processions in which the advocates and proctors took part with the Dean of Arches. Oughton informs us that doctors wear scarlet in the Court of Arches;5 but whereas the Oxford advocates wear their festal robes, the Cambridge advocates use the more formal congregation habit furred with miniver. The doctors take precedence of all barristers, but not of serjeants at law;6 the King's Advocate precedes even the Attorney-General. The author then describes the procedure of the church courts, following a similar scheme to Clarke. Although we are now in Hanoverian England, over 150 years since Clarke was admitted as a proctor, we seem to be in a remarkable time-warp. The proceedings in the church courts might still have been perfectly comprehensible to a visitor from Rome or Salamanca, or to the ghost of Lyndwood, but they were probably more or less incomprehensible to a country clergyman, let alone a warring couple or a harassed executor. Not only the written documents but the oral proceedings were still in Latin and highly ritualistic.7

4 R. Maranta, *De ordine judiciorum* (Venosa, 1570). Maranta died in 1530 or 1540.
5 Black gowns were worn in all the lower courts: P. Floyer, *The Proctor's Practice* (1746 edn), p. 6.
6 This had been a subject of some controversy. But preaudience was only a practical issue in the Court of Delegates, where members of both professions appeared: J. H. Baker, *The Order of Serjeants at Law*, Selden Society, Supplementary Series, 5 (1984), pp. 54–55.
7 The writs and records of the common law were still in Latin also.

Ordo Judiciorum ;

S I V E,

METHODUS PROCEDENDI

I N

Negotiis et Litibus

I N

F O R O Ecclefiaftico-Civili

Britannico et Hibernico.

Ubi, quæ mendis olim cum innumeris edita fuêre, caftigatè nunc et dilucidè digefta, juxta *Normam Ordinis Judiciarii,* exhibentur, ac Notis et Obfervationibus illuftrantur.

Per Thomam Oughton,

Almæ Curiæ Cantuarienfis de Arcubus, London, Procuratorum generalium unum, et à multis retrò Annis Supremæ Curiæ Delegatorum Regiftrarii Regii Deputatum.

L O N D I N I :
Impenfis Authoris.   M.DCC.XXXVIII.

Title-page of the first edition of Oughton's *Ordo judiciorum* (1738).

Oughton's account of the procedure for swearing witnesses to their depositions furnishes a taste of the atmosphere,[8] for which perhaps the only parallel in modern England is in some of the formalities of the ancient universities. When the witnesses appear, the plaintiff's proctor says: 'Produco hos in testes super libello, quos peto recipi et juramento onerari de fideliter deponendo omnem veritatem quam noverint super eodem libello'. If no objection is taken by the other side, the judge responds: 'Admittimus hos testes'. They then place their hands on the Bible, and the judge gives them the oath: 'Jurabitis, et quilibet vestrum jurabit, quod tempore vestrae in hac parte examinationis testificabimini et deponetis, ac quilibet vestrum testificabitur et deponet, omnem et omnimodem veritatem quam noveritis sive noverit; omnibus amore, favore et affectione, necnon omnibus inimicitia, malicia et odio, quae geritis vel gerit quilibet in hac parte litigantibus seu eorum alteri, ac etiam corruptionem generibus quibuscunque penitus semotis; sicut vos et quemlibet vestrum Deus adiuvet et sancta eius evangelia'. The witnesses then kiss the Book, to indicate that they accept the oath. Their testimony has previously been taken down in Latin, a language which (as Clarke had remarked in the 1590s) few witnesses were likely to understand.[9]

This outlandish legal world was a far cry from the common-law assizes, where the presence of juries required at least the oral procedure to be accommodated to the understanding of intelligent laymen. Only a few years after Oughton published his first edition, Parliament abolished the use of Latin in all the courts;[10] and, although this was

---

8 T. Oughton, *Ordo judiciorum*, i, p. 123, tit. 80.

9 Preface to the *Praxis*: 'quos communiter testes (praesertim rustici) non intelligunt'. The duty was cast on the registrar to make sure that the witnesses understood every word that was taken down in Latin.

10 4 Geo. II, c. 26, which took effect from 25 March 1733.

not reflected in the second edition of Oughton, all the forms were thereupon converted, somewhat uncomfortably, into the vernacular. Even after this, however, the cumbersome procedure for taking down written evidence, with no oral cross-examination, was one of the principal reasons for dissatisfaction with the ecclesiastical judicial system.

The new vernacular spirit generated two elementary guides to the practice of the church courts in the middle of the eighteenth century. The first was *The Proctor's Practice in the Ecclesiastical Courts* (1744; second edition, 1746) by Philip Floyer, another Proctor of the Arches.[11] This was an independent work, with some interesting information about the practical workings of the courts, including the first description of the ceremony of admitting an advocate, and a disciplinary order made in Doctors' Commons (1742) concerning proctors' clerks; but it was essentially an outline introduction, not a substitute for Oughton. Of even lighter weight was the Reverend Dr William Cockburn's *The Clerk's Assistant in the Practice of the Ecclesiastical Courts* (1753), though it evidently enjoyed some popularity as preparatory reading, reaching a fifth edition in 1800. In the early nineteenth century, Oughton still continued to hold pride of place as the acknowledged 'oracle of practice' in the ecclesiastical courts.[12]

An attempt was made in 1831 to render Oughton itself more widely accessible. A considerable part of it was translated into English by James Thomas Law, M.A.,[13] Chancellor of Lichfield and Coventry, and printed as *Forms*

11 There was a Dublin edition in 1795, reprinted 1798.
12 A style bestowed on him by Sir William Scott (later Lord Stowell): *Briggs* v. *Morgan* (1820) 3 Phill. Ecc. 325 at 329, where he said that Oughton and Godolphin were 'the oracles of our practice'.
13 Law was not a lawyer. He was the son of George Henry Law († 1845), Bishop of Bath and Wells, to whom the book was dedicated.

of Ecclesiastical Law: or the Mode of Conducting Suits in the Consistory Courts. It included material inserted at the appropriate points from Clarke, Consett and later authors, rendering further recourse to the Latin authors largely unnecessary. But Chancellor Law lamented in the preface that the editorial labour had been so prolonged that 'I can scarcely suffer myself to look forward with any confidence to the completion of the work'. His lack of self-confidence was not misplaced, for the work never was completed. Even so, the first part completely covered procedure in general, and can properly stand alone. For those fortunate enough to find a copy, Chancellor Law's translation, which enjoyed a second edition in 1844, remains the most accessible guide to the classical procedure of the ecclesiastical courts and to the professional traditions passed on by assiduous proctors such as Clarke and Oughton. Those traditions were to be largely destroyed by the drastic reforms of the nineteenth century, which extended to procedure as well as to jurisdiction.

11

Edmund Gibson

LTHOUGH our next two authors were not qualified as lawyers, and had no experience of practice in the ecclesiastical courts, their collections of legal sources have been widely consulted by ecclesiastical lawyers down to the present. Both their endeavours were prompted, indirectly, by a fierce controversy over the constitution of the Church of England and the historic role of Convocation; but, unlike much of the polemical literature spawned by that debate, the works of Gibson and Wilkins each made a more enduring contribution to the history of English ecclesiastical law.

Gibson and his *Codex*

Edmund Gibson was born in the parish of Bampton, Westmoreland, in 1669 and educated at Bampton Grammar School.[1] From school he proceeded to The Queen's College, Oxford, in 1686, becoming a taberdar in 1690 and a fellow in 1696. The college nurtured a group of historians (including William Nicolson and Thomas Tanner) who made their

1 Most of what follows is based on N. Sykes, *Edmund Gibson, Bishop of London, 1669–1748* (Oxford, 1926). This supersedes the brief entry in *DNB*, vii, pp. 1153–54. Cf. [R. Smalbroke], *Some Account of the Rt Reverend Dr Edmund Gibson* (1749). For his political career in the House of Lords, see now S. Taylor, '"Dr Codex" and the Whig "Pope": Edmund Gibson, Bishop of Lincoln and London, 1716–48', in *Lords of Parliament*, ed. R. W. Davis (Stanford, California, 1995), pp. 9–28.

learning available to the Whig cause,[2] especially in the controversy over synodaical government.[3] Gibson commenced his historical studies soon after graduation, and in 1692 completed an edition of the *Saxon Chronicle* begun by William Nicolson. He soon became interested in Roman Britain, and among other publications produced a new translation of Camden's *Britannia* which has been credited with exciting a new academical interest in local history. His work on Camden took him to London, where he stayed with an uncle, and while there he began to muse upon a legal career. He was actually admitted to the Middle Temple in 1694, but within six months he had changed his mind and was back in Oxford preparing for ordination. He was ordained deacon in 1695 and priest in 1697, whereupon – his merits having come to the notice of Archbishop Tenison – he was appointed Librarian of Lambeth Palace, at a salary of £10, and one of the archbishop's personal chaplains. Like his college contemporary Thomas Tanner, Gibson was already an enthusiastic manuscript scholar, keen to locate and catalogue the riches available in English libraries. His *Reliquiae Spelmannianae: The Posthumous Works of Sir Henry Spelman Kt Relating to the Laws and Antiquities of England* (1698) was based on papers he had discovered in London and Norfolk. In the same year was published the monumental *Catalogi manuscriptorum Angliae* to which he had made a major contribution.[4] During this period, however, his

2 Richard Burn, a member of the same college in a later generation, had interests in local history as well as in ecclesiastical law: below, p. 115.

3 Cf. D. M. Owen, *The Medieval Canon Law* (Cambridge, 1990), pp. 60–61, on a wider Oxford grouping. Dr Owen quotes Bishop Stubbs's remark upon them, that 'the very dust of their writings is gold'.

4 It bears the name of Dr Edward Bernard († 1697), the astronomer and bibliophile who acted as editor in chief, but the entries were compiled by different contributors.

position at Lambeth was drawing him into the service of the archbishop in the growing controversy over the Convocation.

The Convocation had not been summoned under Charles II and James II, but in the 1690s some Tory clergymen were making constitutional claims for the Convocation as an ecclesiastical counterpart to Parliament, a body sitting whenever Parliament was in session, and exercising some control over the episcopacy. The bishops, of course, generally preferred to fulfil their burdensome duties without such democratic constraints. The debate became public when a pamphlet war was started in 1697 by Dr Francis Atterbury and Sir Bartholomew Shower K.C., a Bencher of the Middle Temple, who contended that the King had no more right to refuse to call a Convocation than he had to refuse a Parliament. In 1700 William III was prevailed upon by the new ministry to call a Convocation, and warm contention raged in its two houses between then and 1717 when, after an attack by the Lower House on the Bishop of Bangor (Benjamin Hoadly), the Synod was effectively silenced for more than a century. At an early stage in these proceedings Gibson was engaged to investigate the history of Convocation, and he first joined issue with Atterbury in a pamphlet of 1700; he was supported by White Kennett, whose historical treatise on *Ecclesiastical Synods and Parliamentary Convocations in the Church of England* appeared in 1701. In 1702 Gibson began to fulfil his legal aspirations by producing *Synodus anglicana: or The Constitution and Proceedings of an English Convocation*, which he conceived as a non-partisan guide based on precedents.[5]

Although Gibson had furnished material to support the episcopal side of the debate, he regretted the complete disappearance of the Synod in 1717 and made some proposals

5 A new edition, by Cardwell, was printed in 1854.

for reform with a view to its reinstatement. He maintained that the Lower House should be allowed to meet and discuss whatever it saw fit, and to make representations to the Upper House, but he of course resisted the Atterbury position which equated the Lower House with the House of Commons and gave it legislative equality. The dispute had nevertheless, for the time being, become purely academic. It had been academic in another sense, in that it had caused anguish in Oxford. Gibson did not obtain a doctorate from his disgruntled *alma mater* but had to content hmself with a Lambeth D.D. (1702).[6]

Gibson's services to Tenison and the Upper House brought him numerous preferments in the first decade of the eighteenth century: the rectory of Stisted in 1700, a canonry of Chichester in 1703, the rectory of Lambeth in 1704, and the archdeaconry of Surrey in 1710. These enabled him to marry, in 1704, Margaret Jones, daughter of a Shropshire clergyman and sister-in-law of the Dean of Arches.[7] Inspired perhaps by his new role as a family man, Gibson wrote an extremely popular booklet called *Family Devotions* in 1705.[8] Little is known of his own family life, save that there were numerous children.

During the same period, Gibson had been engaged on his *magnum opus*, which was a collection of all 'the statutes, constitutions, canons, rubrics and articles of the Church of England, methodically digested under their proper heads',[9] with the addition of relevant Acts of Parliament and decisions of the common-law courts. The headings were

---

6 For the background, see Sykes, *Edmund Gibson*, pp. 57–58. It occasioned some unresolved questions about the legality of Lambeth degrees.

7 Her sister Elizabeth was the wife of Dr John Bettesworth. Her father was the Rev. John Jones, Rector of Selattyn.

8 18th edn, 1750.

9 From the sub-title to the 1713 edition.

CODEX
JURIS ECCLESIASTICI
ANGLICANI:
OR, THE
STATUTES, CONSTITUTIONS, CANONS, RUBRICKS and ARTICLES,
OF THE
Church of England,
Methodically DIGESTED under their Proper *Heads*.

WITH A
COMMENTARY,
Historical and Juridical.

BEFORE it, is

An Introductory Discourse, concerning the *Present* State of the *Power, Discipline* and *Laws*, of the Church of *England*:

And AFTER it,

An APPENDIX of INSTRUMENTS, Ancient and Modern.

By EDMUND GIBSON, D. D.

Archdeacon of *Surrey*, Rector of *Lambeth*, and Chaplain to his Grace the Lord Archbishop of *Canterbury*.

LONDON:

Printed by *J. Baskett*, Printer to the Queen's Most Excellent Majesty; and by the Assigns of *Thomas Newcomb*, and *Henry Hills*, deceas'd. And are to be Sold by *R. Whitledge*, at the *Bible and Ball* in *Ave-Mary-lane*. 1713.

Gibson's *Codex*, showing the title-page of the 1713 edition.

From a book in the possession of the author

arranged according to the method laid down by Pope
Gregory IX for the ordering of the decretals, and at the end
of each individual text the editor added glosses in smaller
type. By 1710 it was completed, and Gibson sent a specimen
to the Master of University College, Oxford, saying it had
been for many years the employment of his spare hours. It
had been necesary to obtain episcopal approval before publication, and – since publication was to be funded by
subscription – Gibson was worried that this might cause it
to be regarded as a partisan work. In the event it did prove
difficult to recruit subscribers, but by July 1711 there were
enough to satisfy the printers and the book went to press.
It finally appeared in 1713, as *Codex juris ecclesiastici anglicani*, a massive compilation of 1291 pages in two folio
volumes printed by collaboration between the Queen's
Printer (John Baskett) and the patented common-law
printers.[10] In the introduction, Gibson made some contentious claims for the independence of the ecclesiastical courts,
which he placed on an equal footing with the king's temporal
courts, even for the purpose of interpreting Acts of Parliament; and also for the independence of ecclesiastical
authority from lay encroachments, including legislative
measures emanating from Parliament itself.[11] His views in
this respect were outmoded and failed to carry persuasion
to most contemporaries.[12] The body of the work, however,

---

10 CUL, Adv. a. 70.1 is Thomas Tanner's copy, with his notes.
11 Gibson, *Codex*, introduction, pp. xvii–xxxi.
12 See the comments (adverse to Gibson) by Sir William Holdsworth,
History of English Law, xii (1938), pp. 609–10. Some opponents
went so far as to accuse him of high treason for denying the king's
jurisdiction in ecclesiastical matters, though Gibson's argument
was that the ecclesiastical courts were as much the king's courts
as the old courts of common law. A more measured response was
made by Michael Foster (later Mr Justice Foster) in *An Examination of the Scheme of Church Power, Laid Down in the Codex
juris ecclesiastici anglicani* (1735; 5th edn, 1763).

was uncontroversial. It was a painstaking assemblage of texts, including those which had been repealed or were no longer of direct use, these last being included to show 'how the law stood before, and what successive alterations it had undergone'. Even the statute of 1553, re-establishing the papal supremacy under Philip and Mary, found its appropriate place.[13] The scholarship was textual rather than legal, for although Gibson was acquainted in an elementary way with legal sources he seems to have had no substantial knowledge of the old canon law commentators and was doubtless anxious to avoid entering into areas of legal subtlety or complexity. The predominant sources were the provincial constitutions as found in Lyndwood, the Canons of 1603 and post-Reformation Acts of Parliament. Gibson naturally assumed that the clergy could read Latin, and so the old pre-Reformation constitutions were reproduced without benefit of translation.

According to the preface, Gibon's *Codex* was intended 'for the service of the clergy, and in support of the rights and privileges of the Church'. He had no intention of encroaching on the lawyers, who (he said) had their proper place in the conduct of litigation, and in advising on difficult points; but much of the law could be readily understood by clergymen if only they had access to it. Indeed, if the clergy had recourse to the legislation itself, he wrote with some feeling, they would not need to rely on 'persons of mean figure and abilities ... who are no otherwise qualified to direct than as they happen to be possessed of a statute book, and of a talent to talk decisively to those who want one'. Moreover, when the clergy did find it necessary to consult lawyers, they would be able to frame more precise and informed questions if they had read the relevant legislation first. But he added the hope that lawyers also would find it

13 1 & 2 Phil. & Mar., c. 8, printed in Gibson, *Codex*, i, p. 37.

helpful to have all the legislation collected together and set out in such a way that successive changes in the law could easily be seen. Legal history was an essential guide to interpretation, for 'by the sight of all former laws upon the same heads, and such an easy opportunity of comparing them with the laws present, we are let into the true aim and intent of the legislators'. The work might, he admitted modestly, have been better done by a trained lawyer; but lawyers had not so far shown an inclination to do it, and the question was not whether it could have been done better but whether it was better done by him than not at all.

'Dr Codex', as his detractors began to call him,[14] originally intended to use the textual work as the basis for a 'plain analytical system of English Ecclesiastical Law, in the nature of an Institute' which he thought might become a set textbook for ordinands.[15] But the demands soon to be made upon him prevented him from pursuing this plan.[16] In 1716 he was given the see of Lincoln, and in 1723 he was translated to London. By this time he was suffering from ill health, which he blamed on the labour of compiling the *Codex*. He nevertheless managed to survive a quarter of a century of heavy business and political turmoil as Bishop of London, during which period the disciplinary jurisdiction of the ecclesiastical courts over the laity came close to extinction.[17]

---

14 E.g. Anon., *Authentick Memoirs of the Life of Dr Codex* (1725).
15 Gibson, *Codex*, preface, p. viii.
16 Note, however, R. Grey, *A System of English Ecclesiastical Law Extracted from the Codex juris ecclesiastici anglicani* (1730; 2nd edn, 1732; 3rd edn, 1735; 4th edn, 1743), which according to the title-page was intended for 'young students in the universities, who are designed for Holy Orders'. It follows a catechistical method. Richard Grey was Rector of Hinton, Northamptonshire.
17 In 1733 a Bill for removing the *ex officio* jurisdiction of the church courts over the laity, unless the informer undertook to pay the costs, and to entitle defendants to trial by jury, passed the House of Commons but was abandoned in the Lords.

At the age of seventy-nine he was offered the archbishopric of Canterbury, though he was obliged to decline it on grounds of old age and failing health.[18] He died the following year, on 6 September 1748, and was buried at Fulham. An inscription upon his memorial wall-tablet remembers the *Codex* in the following words: 'His Lordship's Peculiar Care and Concern for the Constitution and Discipline of the Church of England were eminently distinguished not only by his Invaluable Collection of Her Laws, but by his prudent and steady Opposition to every Attack made upon Them'.

Gibson had for over thirty years before his death collected notes towards a new edition of the *Codex*, including nine volumes of transcripts of relevant Acts of Parliament passed during that time.[19] There was indeed to be a second edition, but this one and only posthumous edition was the subject of a publishing wrangle revealed by letters now in California.[20] Three years after the bishop's death, his residuary legatees, acting in accordance with what they believed to have been his wishes, authorised the executors to transfer the copyright in the *Codex* to Oxford University Press 'in order to their sending out a new edition of it, with such improvements and additions as he should leave behind him for that purpose', and to hand over all relevant notes in his hand. The Press were to give bonds for its publication by an agreed date. By 1754, however, the right of the Press had been questioned, apparently in the course of a dispute between the relatives,[21] on the ground that the work fell within

---

18 He had been generally expected to succeed Wake in the 1730s, but fell out with Walpole a year before Wake died in 1737.

19 See George Gibson's letter of 1756, quoted below.

20 In the H. E. Huntington Library, San Marino, California, Gibson manuscripts.

21 The nature of the dispute is not clearly revealed by the correspondence. In a letter of 25 November 1754, G. Scott reports to his brother that he is 'heartily sick' of the affair and 'now on very indifferent terms with a near relation of mine', and refers to 'that

the terms of the patent which conferred on Henry Lintot
the monopoly of printing 'all manner of law books which
any way relate to the common or statute law';[22] a contention
which had been supported by an opinion from Mr Randal
Wilbraham, a Bencher of Lincoln's Inn. The Press were
unwilling to delegate the printing, or to dispute the patent,
and instead offered to print the edition and give Lintot thirty
copies as compensation. These terms seem to have been
acceptable to Lintot, and an agreement was on the point of
being sealed when a young don called William Blackstone
intervened to point out that the university's rights under its
charter overrode general patent rights such as Lintot's.[23] On
31 December 1755 a revised publishing agreement was drawn
up between the university, George Gibson (as executor) and
Thomas Baskett, the King's Printer,[24] to print an edition of
Codex juris ecclesiastici anglicani within twelve months. In
March 1756, George Gibson reported to Oxford that in
accordance with their agreement he had delivered the *Codex*
to a solicitor, Robert Palmer, adding:

> It will, Sir, be observed that there are only 4 folio volumes
> that have the title of Codex, the other nine volumes
> are a collection of acts relative to the Church and two

---

very extraordinary piece of advice of the late Dean of the Arches'.
This last was Dr Bettesworth, the husband of Bishop Gibson's
wife's sister, and one of the bishop's executors.

22 For the troubled history of the patent, see W. M. Sale, *Samuel
Richardson: Master Printer* (Ithaca, New York, 1950), pp. 134–44.
The sole printing of statutes belonged to the King's Printer, though
he seems never to have staked a claim to synodal legislation.

23 See H. Carter, ed., *A History of the Oxford University Press*, i
(Oxford, 1975), pp. 332–33. Cf. *Basket* v. *University of Cambridge*
(1758) 1 Wm Bla. 105.

24 The King's Printer had the monopoly of printing statutes, and
the *Codex* included a number of statutory texts. However, Baskett
was content with one copy as a formal acknowledgment of his
interest.

universitys which the Bishop intended as an appendix to a new edition of this work, and as you have receaved Mr Baskett's consent it can not but be of great consequence to have them preserved and digested into their respective dioceses as is already done in the 3 large folios, and in order to make the collections as compleat as may be would it not be very proper to desire Mr Basket to furnish you with all the publick and private acts relative to the Church or University since the year 1747? To which time the Bishop was very punctual in procuring them as they respectively passed.

The edition finally appeared in 1761. Five hundred copies were printed, of which only 150 were sold in the first ten years.[25] The small demand accounts for the absence of any further edition, though the work is still sought after by those who study or practise ecclesiastical law and a facsimile edition was published in 1969. Its principal value lies in the convenience of being able to find under alphabetical heads the ecclesiastical and parliamentary legislation governing the Church of England up to the date of publication, though it is as well to remember that the texts which it contains are of no special authority and have been almost entirely superseded by later editions. Gibson's additions, in the form of brief commentaries on each text, though perhaps lacking in originality,[26] are of independent value and even authority. High praise, moreover, was bestowed upon the preface and introduction by the Archbishops' Commission of 1939–47, which went so far as to declare it the best

25 Carter, ed., *History of the Oxford University Press*, i, p. 333. Copies of the 1713 edition seem to be more readily found even today, though the 1761 edition has been reprinted in facsimile (Farnborough, 1969).

26 Cf. Sykes, *Edmund Gibson*, p. 71: 'Although devoid of originality and imagination, he was at his best in the patient and minute research which such a publication demanded'.

account available of the sources of the law of the church, 'absolutely indispensable to any serious student of the law and constitution of the Church of England'.[27]

As a collection of source material, the *Codex* is open to the objection that shredding the texts and sifting them into headings removes them from their original context. Moreover, in the absence of a translation, there is little guidance to difficulties of interpretation. An attempt to remedy these deficiencies, on a less lavish scale, was made by the Reverend John Johnson (1662–1725), Vicar of Cranbrook in Kent. His *Collection of Ecclesiastical Laws*, published in two volumes in 1720, contained a new English translation of the constitutions from Anglo-Saxon times as far as the Reformation, and also paraphrased selected glosses from Ayton and Lyndwood.[28] One of Johnson's avowed aims was 'to furnish out a strong Antidote against Popery', which could best be done by revealing the old texts in a language which everyone could understand. He nevertheless makes the point that, as a result of the statute of 1534,[29] the lawful pre-Reformation constitutions were of greater force than the Canons of 1603, which had no statutory force.[30] His conclusion was that a thorough overhaul of the ecclesiastical law by Convocation was overdue. The book is a careful collection of texts from Lyndwood and Spelman, adding nothing new but taking

27 *The Canon Law of the Church of England* (London, 1947), p. 55. Cf. Owen, *Medieval Canon Law*, p. 61, who says that it is 'still of use to the modern scholar, a point on which Professor Cheney did not agree with me'.

28 J. Johnson, *A Collection of All the Ecclesiastical Laws, Canons, Answers, or Rescripts, with Other Memorials Concerning the Government, Discipline and Worship of the Church of England, from its First Foundation to the Conquest ... and of All the Canons and Constitutions Ecclesiastical, Made since the Conquest before the Reformation* (1720; new edn, Oxford, 1850–51).

29 25 Hen. VIII, c. 19; quoted above, p. 54.

30 Johnson, *Ecclesiastical Laws*, introduction, p. xxx.

pains to correct errors and suggest emendations with a view
to producing a translation which made sense. It is still useful
– save perhaps to those able to read abbreviated Latin as
easily as they read English – and especially so since there is
a straightforward subject-index; it is, however, scarce.[31]

Edmund Gibson (1669–1748), Bishop of London, c. 1735. Line engraving by Reading after
a painting by John Vanderbank, published in
1820.

From a print in the possession of the author

31 A new edition was published in the Library of Anglo-Catholic
Theology (Oxford, 1850–51).

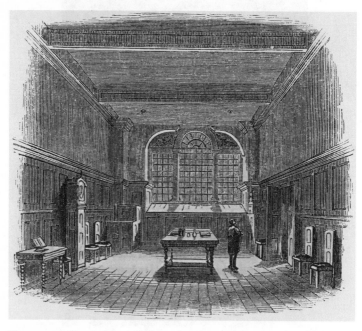

Vestry room in St Mary-le-Bow, London, where the Court of Arches used to sit. Woodcut from C. Knight, *London*, vol. v, part ci.

12

David Wilkins

 LMOST contemporary with Gibson, and like him a scholarly collector of legal texts, was David Wilkins.[1] Wilkins, however, came from a very different background. Born in Prussia in 1685, with the family name of Wilke, he travelled the Continent as a wandering student, immersing himself in languages ancient and modern. In his twenties he settled in England, continuing his studies at Oxford, and Anglicised his surname. He was ordained in 1711 and attracted the attention of Thomas Tenison, Archbishop of Canterbury, who appointed him to succeed Gibson as Librarian of Lambeth Palace in 1715. Tenison and his successor William Wake procured various benefices for his support, and Wake appointed him one of his chaplains in 1719. Although his principal occupation in these years was that of a professional record searcher and transcriber, he was clearly a scholar of some standing. Admittedly Oxford declined to accept his qualifications for the degree of M.A., but Cambridge made good the omission, first by creating him doctor of divinity in 1717 and then, in 1724, by appointing him Professor of Arabic. Notwithstanding his reputation as a philologist, his main enthusiasm seems to have been for early legal history and he is remembered today chiefly for the works which he edited in that connection.

---

1 Biographical information from *DNB*, xxi, pp. 260–61 (biography by J. M. Rigg).

In 1721 Wilkins brought out an edition of *Leges Anglo-Saxonicae ecclesiasticae et civiles*, which held the field until 1840. It included also some Anglo-Norman texts, Sir Henry Spelman's edition of the statutes from William I to Henry III, and William Nicolson's dissertation on Saxon feudal law. No doubt his oriental as well as his legal interests combined to draw him to the scholarship of John Selden, and in 1725 he produced the only complete edition of Selden's works, in three folio volumes.[2] But his best-known work was his edition of the provincial legislation of the English church from the earliest times up to the last Convocation of 1717.

The *Concilia Magnae Britanniae et Hiberniae a Synodo Verolamiensi A.D. 446 ad Londinensem A.D. 1717* appeared in four large volumes in 1737, with a fulsome Latin dedication to King George II. A letter dated 1733, also prefaced to the first volume, acknowledges the patronage of Archbishop Wake. The researches of Professor Jacob uncovered a good deal of the background to the edition.[3] Wake does indeed seem to have been the moving force behind the project, and the context was the same controversy over synodaical government that gave rise to Gibson's *Codex*. In writing his *State of the Church and Clergy of England* (1703), Wake had compiled several volumes of transcripts, and over the next twenty years or so he employed Wilkins to augment his collection. Twenty-four of Wake's volumes remain in the library of Christ Church, Oxford, and they include one written in Wilkins's hand and others with notes by him. Wilkins's own historical collections passed after his death in 1745 to his wife's family, the Fairfaxes of Leeds Castle

---

2 *Seldeni opera omnia* (1725, 1726).

3 E. F. Jacob, 'Wilkins's *Concilia* and the Fifteenth Century', *Transactions of the Royal Historical Society*, fourth series, 15 (1931), pp. 91–131.

in Kent,4 from whom they were acquired by Sir Thomas
Phillipps in the early nineteenth century; but they were dispersed at auction in 1898.5

The idea of a published collection of legislative and constitutional documents was Wake's, and it is credibly
supposed that he had first entrusted the edition to Dr John
Walker, who abandoned the task when he found himself
unable to cope with the Anglo-Saxon. A letter from Thomas
Tanner to Wilkins in November 1732, concerning what he
called the latter's 'noble work', suggests that its precise scope
was still unsettled.6 Nevertheless, it is clear that the scheme
was essentially to produce a new edition of Spelman's *Concilia* and to extend it to modern times. The intention of Sir
Henry Spelman († 1641) had been to extend Lyndwood
backwards from 1222 to Anglo-Saxon times, though he lived
to see only the pre-1066 portion in print.7 A continuation
by Sir William Dugdale († 1686) had been published in 1664,
though most of the copies were destroyed in the Great Fire
of 1666. Dugdale planned a third volume in the series, and
some of his collections survive, though it did not materi-
alise.8 In the event, Wilkins's *Concilia* incorporated all of
Spelman's material, including even his essay on the origins
of the British church, and thereby rendered Spelman's separate book obsolete. Wilkins also extended Lyndwood

---

4 Wilkins married Mary, daughter of Lord Fairfax, in 1725. He
   died at Hadleigh, in Suffolk, where he was rector, on 6 September
   1745.
5 Bodleian Library, Oxford, MS C. 64 is a Spelman collection, with
   additions by Tanner, which passed to Wilkins.
6 Bodleian Library, Oxford, MS Autog. C. 8, fo. 13, printed in
   Proceedings of the British Academy, 16 (1931), p. 377.
7 H. Spelman, *Concilia, decreta, leges, consuetudines in re ecclesia-
   rum orbis britannici* (1639).
8 For the history of this work, see F. M. Powicke, 'Sir Henry Spelman and the *Concilia*', *Proceedings of the British Academy*, 16
   (1931), pp. 345–79; also printed separately, as a Raleigh Lecture.

forwards by adding the constitutions and canons down to the enactments of the last Synod in 1717, and for good measure incorporated a good deal of miscellaneous non-legal material relating to the history and constitution of the church, some of it in abridged form.

The *Concilia* has generally been praised as a monumental work of scholarship, impressive for its time. But it became increasingly inadequate for the more exacting medieval historians of the nineteenth and twentieth centuries. Far fewer manuscripts were accessible in 1737 than nowadays: for example, while Wilkins used four texts of the constitutions of the Council of Oxford (1222), fifty are now known. Anglo-Saxon studies were still in their infancy in the 1730s, and some of Wilkins's transcriptions and translations of earlier materials were faulty. Irish and Celtic materials were omitted altogether. Wilkins was generally an accurate transcriber of Latin texts, though he did not always collate the various manuscripts which he cited. A more serious criticism is that he did not bring a historian's judgment to bear on his evidence. He could not always set his materials in a correct sequence or chronological context, and he was apt to detach documents from a larger series in such a way as to create a misleading impression of their overall content. Nor did Wilkins have the same interest in law or procedure as Gibson, and the book was apparently conceived of as an adjunct to church history rather than as a resource for ecclesiastical lawyers.

The first attempt to replace Wilkins was made by Haddan and Stubbs in 1869.[9] They modestly claimed merely to be attempting 'a reproduction of that great work in accordance with the present state of our knowledge and materials', and

9 A. W. Haddan and W. Stubbs, *Councils and Ecclesiastical Documents Relating to Great Britain and Ireland* (Oxford, 1869), in three volumes.

conceded that without Wilkins their endeavour would have been impossible. But they did not mince words:

> it is no imputation either upon that indefatigable scholar's industry, or upon his critical skill, to say, that for our present needs, and with our present materials, and according to the sounder canons of present historical and philological knowledge, his work is inadequate, exceedingly defective and incomplete, and (especially in the earlier portions) uncritical; to say nothing of the not few blemishes which disfigure it ...

Their own edition replaced Wilkins for the earliest period, and the remainder was overtaken by further scholarship in the present century. Sir Maurice Powicke proposed a new edition of the texts and, after many years of labour by his erstwhile pupil Professor Christopher Cheney, a new edition for the period 1205–1313 appeared in 1964.[10] The edition has since been carried back to A.D. 871.[11] All three projects adopted different principles of selection, the most recent excluding non-legislative material such as capitular statutes, statutes governing courts and episcopal *acta*. It is therefore still necessary to have occasional recourse to Wilkins for printed texts of the more miscellaneous material contained in it. But Wilkins's contribution to ecclesiastical law, a subject in which he was not trained or particularly interested, must now be deemed spent.

10 *Councils and Synods with Other Documents Relating to the English Church*, ii, *1205–1313*, ed. F. M. Powicke and C. R. Cheney (Oxford, 1964), issued in two volumes.
11 *Councils and Synods with Other Documents Relating to the English Church*, i, *871–1204*, ed. D. Whitelock, M. Brett and C. N. L. Brooke (Oxford, 1981), issued in two volumes. This instalment was, most regrettably, printed from typescript copy.

The Courtroom in Doctors' Commons, showing the Court of Arches in session before Sir William Wynne, Dean of Arches, in 1808. The advocates, in scarlet, stand at the bar on either side of the judge, and the proctors (in black gowns with miniver-faced hoods) sit at the table below them. The room was built around 1671, and demolished in 1867; the oval plaques on the wall depicted the arms of members of Doctors' Commons from 1709. Hand-coloured aquatint by Rowlandson and Pugin, from R. Ackermann, *Microcosm of London*.

From a print in the possession of the author

13

Richard Burn

E have arrived, now, in the century of Richard Burn (1709–85), who at the present day is perhaps more widely known than any of the writers so far mentioned.[1] In turning to Burn and his famous book on ecclesiastical law, we may begin with the observation that at the time of writing the first edition he was, in legal terms, a layman. He graduated from the Queen's College, Oxford, but instead of reading law took Orders and became a parish priest as Vicar of Orton in Westmorland – a mere ten miles from Edmund Gibson's birthplace – where he remained for the rest of his life. A native of Westmorland, he took a keen interest in its antiquities and helped to write the principal county history.[2] In what must have been ample time for leisure by modern standards,[3] he also turned to

---

1 Brief biography by T. Cooper in *DNB*, iii, pp. 377–78; *Biographical Dictionary of the Common Law*, ed. Simpson, pp. 89–90 (entry by D. E. C. Yale). See also Holdsworth, *History of English Law*, xii, pp. 332–34, 612–13.

2 *The History and Antiquities of the Counties of Westmorland and Cumberland* (1777), two volumes, was written jointly with Joseph Nicolson.

3 He was not the only learned clergyman in the eighteenth century to write on ecclesiastical law. See also H. Prideaux, *Directions to Churchwardens* (1701; 10th edn, 1835) and J. Johnson, *The Clergyman's Vade Mecum* (1706); *Collection of All Ecclesiastical Laws* (1720), above, p. 106. Humphrey Prideaux († 1724) was a D.D., but is best remembered as an orientalist: *DNB*, xvi, pp. 352–54. For the questioned attribution of W. Watson, *Clergyman's Law* (1701), see above, p. 77 n. 1.

private legal study, perhaps stimulated by his service as a country justice. Certainly he was best known in his own day as the author of *Justice of the Peace*, which was first published in 1755. Burn's *Justice* rapidly became the standard manual for magistrates. It was arranged alphabetically, for ready reference, but was far superior to an abridgment since, within each heading, the treatment was discursive and explanatory. The book enjoyed a deserved success, and reached a thirtieth (and last) edition in 1869. Burn was so highly thought of, as a result of this success, that he was engaged to edit the first posthumous edition of Blackstone; this appeared in 1783, but Burn's only additions were those necessitated by recent Acts of Parliament. His name was retained on the tenth and eleventh editions (of 1786 and 1791), but by then he was himself dead and the editing was done by John Williams (later Serjeant Williams).

It was doubtless the success of his *Justice*, coupled with his ecclesiastical interests, which led Burn to apply the same technique to the law concerning the church. *Ecclesiastical Law*, the second of his best-sellers, appeared in 1763.[4] In both endeavours, he acknowledged the help and instruction of Dr Waugh, Dean of Worcester, and Thomas Simpson, Clerk of the Peace for Cumberland.[5] John Waugh's influence is easy to account for; he was likewise a member of the Queen's College, slightly senior to Burn, and had been Chancellor of Carlisle.[6]

---

4 Some reference books (including *DNB*) mention a first edition of 1760, but this seems to be a ghost. Burn also published a *Digest of the Militia Laws* in 1760, and a *History of the Poor Laws* in 1764. A posthumous publication of little merit, edited by his son John, was *A New Law Dictionary* (1792); this has an engraved portrait of Dr Burn (see opposite).

5 End of preface to *Ecclesiastical Law*. Thomas Simpson, Clerk of the Peace 1728–68, was an attorney (adm. 1730): E. Stephens, *The Clerks of the Counties, 1360–1960* (1961), p. 72.

6 J. Foster, *Alumni Oxonienses, 1715–1886* (Oxford, 1892), iv, p. 1513. Waugh († 1765) was Dean of Worcester, 1751–65.

Richard Burn D.C.L. (1709-85), Chancellor of the Diocese of Carlisle. Line engraving by Thomas Trotter, published by T. Cadell, 1 Dec. 1791.

From a copy of Burn's New Law Dictionary in the Inner Temple Library

The only professional ecclesiastical lawyer whose help Burn acknowledged was Dr Topham, Judge of the Prerogative Court at York (and, as such, successor to Swinburne).7 Burn took the degree of doctor of civil law in 1762, doubtless on the strength of the manuscript of *Ecclesiastical Law*; and three years later, armed with this legal qualification, he himself became Chancellor of Carlisle. But the work had been written without benefit of law degree or court experience, and perhaps the clarity of an outsider's vision was an advantage, at any rate when that outsider was a careful scholar with a lawyer's attention to distinctions of principle.

With the publication of Burn's *Ecclesiastical Law*, the law of the English church finally approached the standard of elegant literature. Indeed, the style is almost Blackstonian in its classical grace and clarity, though it can hardly be supposed that either writer had much opportunity to influence the other. The original edition is in two quarto volumes,8 with a dedication to King George III. In the preface Burn treats of the sources of ecclesiastical law, which he holds to be compounded of 'four main ingredients': the civil law of Rome, the canon law (meaning the pre-Reformation *Corpus iuris canonici*, together with the legatine and provincial constitutions, and the Canons of 1603), the common law, and statute law. The mention of civil law may seem rather anachronistic. Burn, though not himself a civilian, makes the traditional acknowledgment that 'there is no understanding the canon law without being very well versed in the civil law'. However, there is little further reference to it. The four kinds of source, according

---

7 Francis Topham († 1770) was a Cambridge man, having taken his LL.D. from Sidney Sussex College; he was admitted an advocate of the Arches in 1747, and practised at York: J. and J. A. Venn, *Alumni Cantabrigienses to 1751* (Cambridge, 1927), iv, p. 253; Squibb, *Doctors' Commons*, p. 192.

8 From 1767, it was published in four octavo volumes.

to Burn, followed the same order of precedence: in case of conflict, 'The Civil Law submitteth to the Canon law; both of these to the Common law; and all three to the Statute law'. The writer added for completeness that courts of equity sometimes touched upon matters of canon law, as in matrimonial and testamentary matters. Referring to his authorities, Burn says:

In citing authorities, the author hath deemed it indispensable, to attribute to every man what is his own; having often observed, not without some degree of indignation, authors of great name borrowing from others without acknowledging the debt. Therefore he alledgeth his vouchers upon all occasions, of what credit soever they be; endeavouring at the same time, not to lay more burden upon any one than he can very well bear ...

A work composed of such a variety of materials, cannot in any respect be satisfactory, without searching the foundations; consequently, it hath been endeavoured to represent not only the law, but the history of that law, in its several gradations, from its first beginning under the christian emperors till its arrival in England, from thence, during the Danish and Saxon periods, to the Norman conquest; from the Norman conquest to the reformation; and from the reformation to the present time ...

It is to be lamented, that amongst the professors of the civil and canon law on the one hand, and of the common law on the other, so little of candour is to be found; inasmuch that it may be laid down as one good general rule of interpretation, that what a common lawyer voucheth for the church, and a canonist or civilian voucheth against it, is for that reason of so much the greater authority.

Contrary judgments, according to the different

measures of right in the several courts, are another cause of regret. And not seldom the determinations in the same court have been various. For tho' truth is still the same, yet the apprehensions of men concerning it are different. And this must unavoidably, so far, be the parent of uncertainty.

One thing further is to be noted, that in all the books of this kind there is a distasteful intermixture of latin and english throughout; occasioned by the Roman civil and canon laws ... being written in the latin tongue: These the author hath taken the liberty to exhibit in an english literal translation ...9

The body of the work is alphabetically arranged, from *Abbot* to *Wills*, with entries of widely varying lengths. Considerable use was made of previous works, particularly Gibson's *Codex*. Since attention has been drawn to a passage in Godolphin concerning the office of chancellor,10 it is instructive to compare Burn on the subject.11 Burn sets out the previous learning, and mentions Dr Sutton's case, but adds that that case was more recently denied to be law, in the case of Dr Jones, Chancellor of Llandaff. He then quotes Bishop Stillingfleet on the distinction between contentious and 'voluntary' jurisdiction, as bearing on the question how far a bishop retains powers of jurisdiction in his own person, and also on the tenure of the office of chancellor. This essay owes much to Gibson, and makes no reference to writers on canon law before the eighteenth century. Nevertheless, there is nothing of substance in the earlier writers which is not touched upon and elegantly disposed of. This is characteristic of the work as a whole. Very few sources are cited

9 Burn, *Ecclesiastical Law* (1763), i, pp. xx–xxi.
10 See above, p. 83.
11 Burn, *Ecclesiastical Law* (1763), i, pp. 208–10, tit. 'Chancellors, &c.'.

which were published before 1700, and even in the common-law sphere the plethora of new reports furnished illustrations of most points without recourse to the older black-letter books; on the other hand, little is omitted which might conceivably be of current value, except of the more intensely practical nature. In addition to titles which had become conventional by his time, Burn included some new topics, including an extensive survey of university law (tit. 'Colleges') and primary education ('Schools'), sections on church property (e.g. 'Leases'), essays on 'Holidays', the 'Kalendar', and divine service (e.g. 'Public Worship'), and notes on other churches (e.g. 'Dissenters', 'Jews', 'Popery', and even 'Mahometans'). In accordance with the decision to concentrate on matters of current utility, the largest single title, containing over 250 pages, is the last ('Wills').

The work was extremely successful, and passed through a number of editions. In the sixth edition (1797), by Simon Fraser († 1803), barrister of the Inner Temple, it was embellished with some references to the *Corpus iuris canonici*; in the seventh (1809) some notes by Mr Serjeant Hill were inserted. After an eighth edition (1824), by Robert Philip Tyrwhitt (1798–1836), student of the Middle Temple,[12] and an epitome (1840) by Francis James Newman Rogers Q.C. († 1851), Bencher of the Inner Temple,[13] it reached its final form in 1842 when it was belatedly taken over by a practising civilian. The ninth edition by Dr (later Sir Robert) Phillimore was a considerably enlarged version of Fraser's, augmented

---

12 Tyrwhitt was not called to the Bar until the following year (1825). He was subsequently a metropolitan magistrate, and is better remembered for his Exchequer reports.

13 F. J. N. Rogers, *A Practical Arrangement of Ecclesiastical Law* (1840; 2nd edn, 1849). This was, as Phillimore remarked (preface to the 9th edn of Burn, *Ecclesiastical Law*, p. vii) 'destined for the circuit', and was of no independent value. Rogers was Deputy Judge Advocate-General, 1842–51.

not only with extensive notes but with a number of new chapters, including sections on the legal status of the church in Ireland and Scotland, and in the colonies and foreign dominions, the practice of the courts in Doctors' Commons, the ecclesiastical commissioners, the Marriage Acts, chaplains, and the councils of the church. Some statutes and judgments were inserted verbatim, for ease of reference. Dr Phillimore expressed the hope that the book would be useful to clergy as well as lawyers, and that both would profit from the historical notes he had added. In his industrious hands the 1842 edition was beginning to take on a new character, and may indeed be regarded as a transition towards the well-known works which Phillimore later composed in his own right.[14]

In places Burn is no more than an abridgment, with strings of only loosely related authorities. But usually the author has imposed some continuity on the materials, and has made them readable in sequence. Though conceived as a reference book, it is a book in which each title can be read through as a coherent piece. Holdsworth justly summarised Burn's achievement by saying that his learning 'and his gift of clear exposition, enabled him to write the clearest and most successful of all the great treatises upon English ecclesiastical law'.[15] Burn's success may, indeed, have contributed indirectly to the decline of Doctors' Commons by making their branch of learning seem more accessible. Yet his own doctorate should not mislead us into thinking of him as a civilian. He had learned his law in the first instance as a serving magistrate, and had learned his ecclesiastical law largely from printed books in English and from the law reports of the common law. His methodology, therefore, was in essence that of a common lawyer. He wanted modern

14 See below, p. 155.
15 Holdsworth, *History of English Law*, xii, p. 613.

cases rather than antiquated Latin texts, and he lamented the absence of reports of cases in the ecclesiastical courts. The effect of this gap in legal literature is apparent in his emphasis on the case-law of the common-law courts and the techniques which it enshrined.

In fact, some of the advocates in Doctors' Commons had been keeping reports of cases for their own private use,[16] but they did not print them,[17] and as a result the jurisprudence to which they contributed made little impact on the printed books of ecclesiastical law. Perhaps the advocates thought their specialist knowledge would be more valued if it was not generally available. But we should be slow to blame the doctors – whether for indolence or for a conscious decision to withhold publication – since it was unclear at that period whether there was a large enough market to justify printing ecclesiastical law reports at all.[18] Their learning no doubt surpassed Burn's, in that they apparently continued to preserve in their practice the cosmopolitan traditions of earlier centuries, and they were in addition the

16 E. g. Dr Trumbull's (c. 1668–73) in CUL, MS Add. 8866 (succession cases); Dr Sayer's (1714–28) in Lincoln's Inn, MS Misc. 147; Dr Lee's (1752–58), next note; Dr Burrell's (1765–69) in Kansas University, MS E181. For some pre-1640 anonymous reports, see R. H. Helmholz, *Roman Canon Law in Reformation England* (Cambridge, 1990), pp. 198–99.

17 Only one series (Dr George Lee's) has been printed, in an edition of 1832–33. The autograph reports from 1752 to 1754 (in four volumes), together with his commonplace books, accounts and other manuscripts, were sold by the representatives of Dr John Lee († 1866) at Sotheby's in Noveber 1888, lots 424–37, and dispersed. Cf. E. W. Kemp, *An Introduction to Canon Law in the Church of England* (1957), p. 42. Sayer's reports (last note) were from the same collection, lot 404. It would good to have modern editions of Sayer and Burrell.

18 The first venture of this kind was Dr Joseph Phillimore's (1818), rapidly followed by Haggard and Addams. This was some thirty years after the establishment of regular reporting in Westminster Hall.

guardians of a recondite system of procedure; but, in the absence of any printed record of their arguments and decisions, their jurisprudence was destined to fade as human memories evaporated and greater reliance was placed on the printed word. To many outside their world, including the practitioners of the common law, printed books of the calibre of Burn, referring them to accessible English cases and authorities, may have seemed adequate in themselves. Anybody with legal acumen could now be a passable ecclesiastical lawyer when occasion arose, and the raison d'être of a separate profession of canonists became less obvious. The old kind of ecclesiastical law thus suffered a mortal infection from the common law and its methodology nearly a century before the fatal reforms of the 1850s.

George Lee D.C.L. (1701–58), President of Doctors' Commons, 1751–58. Mezzotint by Faber after a painting by J. Wills, showing the scarlet Oxford robes as worn by advocates in the Court of Arches.

14

Stephen Lushington

EFORE the coup de grâce was administered to the civilian advocates in 1857, Doctors' Commons enjoyed a final flowering in the Georgian period, when its leading members once again achieved a reputation for scholarship and intellectual distinction. Lord Eldon's brother, William Scott (1745–1836), Lord Stowell, undoubtedly bears a considerable part of the credit for raising the public standing of the civilian profession. Scott was a remarkable man, and his career far from conventional. Fellow and Tutor of University College, Oxford, at the age of nineteen – in the very year that his neighbour Blackstone across the High became Vinerian Professor – he was called to the Bar by the Middle Temple the year after proceeding doctor of civil law, and by 1794 was both a bencher of his inn and a distinguished ecclesiastical judge. Yet not only was Dr Scott a civilian and a barrister; he also taught for several years at Oxford, as Reader in Ancient History, and served as a Member of Parliament. In law and in politics, Stowell shared the conservative instincts of his brother. While professing to value the principle of religious toleration, he was strenuously opposed to Roman Catholic emancipation in Ireland, which he felt would be 'setting fire to the country', while in the Commons in 1815 he urged that sectarians should not be excused from contributing to the maintenance of the established church. In a letter to Joseph Story in 1820 he explained his opposition to all manner of reform, including moderate reform – the latter

he considered particularly dangerous, because a modest reform was easily made and then the violent reformers would
rush into the breach.[1]

Stowell was not a gifted extempore speaker. An American
visitor to his court in 1819 was surprised to find that 'his
elocution did not appear to me the best; his manner was
hesitating; his sentences more than once got entangled, and
his words were sometimes recalled that others might be
substituted'.[2] Yet his prepared lectures at Oxford were
accounted brilliant, and his written judgments met with
universal praise. We know that the choice of words and
phrases plagued him beyond the moment of delivery, because
the same American writer was informed that 'not only would
he change words while the opinion was in the press, but
reconstruct whole sentences', and that on one occasion,
'after an anxious correction of the proof sheet, and a revise
after that, the type was nearly all pulled down to be set up
again for some better transposition of the sentences'.[3] Lord
Brougham – a political adversary – said of his judicial work:
'His judgment was of the higher caste, endowed with all the
learning and capacity which can accomplish, as well as the
graces which can embellish, the judicial character. It was
calm, firm, enlarged, penetrating, profound. If ever the
praise of being luminous could be bestowed on human composition, it was upon his judgments.'[4]

1 Quoted in H. J. Bourguignon, *Sir William Scott, Lord Stowell,
Judge of the High Court of Admiralty, 1798–1828* (Cambridge,
1987), at p. 52. The information about Scott is taken from Bourguignon, and from the article in *DNB*, xvii, pp. 1046–50 by
J. A. Hamilton (later Lord Sumner).
2 R. Rush, *Residence at the Court of London: Comprising Incidents,
Official and Personal, from 1819 to 1825* (Philadelphia, 1845), i,
p. 15.
3 Ibid., pp. 15–16.
4 H. Brougham, *Statesmen of the Time of George III* (1872 edn),
iv, p. 67.

Stowell is nowadays remembered primarily as an Admiralty judge,5 but many of his judgments in ecclesiastical cases were reported, including those in *Evans* v. *Evans* and *Dalrymple* v. *Dalrymple* on the nature of marriage,6 and that in *Gilbert* v. *Buzzard* – the case of the iron coffin – which settled the physical requirements of lawful burial.7 In these cases the institutions of marriage and burial were characteristically traced from the earliest Classical times, and comparisons drawn from different countries and religious persuasions. Such learning could not be left to evaporate in the memory, and it can hardly be a mere coincidence that the practice of publishing reports of Admiralty and ecclesiastical cases was belatedly started around this time. The civilian profession during the time of Stowell's dominance attracted men of the quality of Christopher Robinson (1796), Joseph Phillimore (1804), Jesse Addams (1811), John Haggard (1818) and William Curteis (1826), all of whom became law reporters;8 Herbert Jenner (1803) (later Sir Herbert Jenner-Fust) and John Dodson (1808), who each became Dean of Arches; and John Lee (1816), who was to lead the unsuccessful fight to save Doctors' Commons in the 1860s.9

Dr Stephen Lushington (1782–1873) entered this select

5 E. S. Roscoe, *Lord Stowell: His Life and the Development of English Prize Law* (1916); Bourguignon, *Lord Stowell, Judge of the High Court of Admiralty* (above, p. 126).

6 *Evans* v. *Evans* (1790) 1 Hag. Con. 35; *Dalrymple* v. *Dalrymple* (1811) 2 Hag. Con. 54 (validity of a secret marriage contracted informally in Scotland).

7 *Gilbert* v. *Buzzard* (1821) 3 Phill. Ecc. 335, 2 Hag. Con. 333.

8 Robinson's reports, however, were confined to Admiralty cases. Some manuscript ecclesiastical reports by Dr Parson, from the first decade of the nineteenth century, were sold by the representatives of Dr John Lee († 1866) at Sotheby's in November 1888, lot 558. Part of the autograph of Dr Joseph Phillimore's reports was in the same sale (lot 565).

9 See further below, p. 144.

group in 1808.[10] A Fellow of All Souls since 1801, he had
at first intended a political career and was called to the Bar
by the Inner Temple in 1806. (Like Stowell, he was to become
a Bencher of his inn, a distinction rare for civilians.) He did
indeed serve in Parliament, but he lacked the subservience
and the willingness to compromise which are necessary to
attain place, and turned instead to the study and practice
of the civil law. This turn in his career was no doubt sug-
gested by his father, Sir Stephen Lushington, Bt, who had
been a proctor before becoming Chairman of the East India
Company.[11] Dr Lushington succeeded in due course of time
to Stowell's offices of Judge of the Consistory Court of
London (1828) and Judge of the Admiralty Court (1838),
becoming finally Dean of the Arches (1858). Though he was
a great admirer of Stowell, before whom he practised for
many years, a more different personality can hardly be im-
agined.

As a keen supporter of religious toleration and Roman
Catholic emancipation,[12] an opponent of the slave trade and
of capital and corporal punishment, Lushington was generally as warm in the cause of reform as Stowell was in resisting

10 The following essay on Dr Lushington is based almost entirely
on S. M. Waddams, *Law, Politics and the Church of England: The
Career of Stephen Lushington, 1782–1873* (Cambridge, 1992), to
which the present writer is heavily indebted and to which the
reader is referred for further and better particulars. Professor
Waddams is now engaged on a history of the defamation jurisdiction of the ecclesiastical courts in the nineteenth century.

11 Squibb, *Doctors' Commons*, p. 198; *DNB*, xii, p. 291. The name
Stephen was widely used in the family. There was another contemporary M.P. called Stephen Lushington († 1868), who was
given an honorary D.C.L. (Oxon.) in 1839, and another Sir
Stephen Lushington († 1877), who commanded the naval brigade
at Sevastopol and became an admiral: *DNB*, xii, p. 293.

12 This was one of the reasons for his support of the founding of
London University (i.e. what is now University College London).
He was a proprietor, and member of the council.

it. Moreover, his reforming zeal did not stop short at the entry to Knightrider Street. He was deeply sensitive to the manifold criticisms of the spiritual jurisdiction, which reached their climax in 1846 with the formation of a Society for the Abolition of Ecclesiastical Courts as 'a source of oppression and hardship, and a national dishonour'. Lushington did not accept the wildest of these censures, but he was not a man to bestow his talents upon the defence of any institution which upon sincere reflection he found wanting, out of mere professional loyalty: to permit perceived defects to continue could only harm the Church of England itself. And, as things turned out, Lushington's destiny was indirectly to facilitate the extinction of the profession he had himself chosen in 1808.

In 1830, as one of the most senior ecclesiastical judges in the country, Dr Lushington was appointed to the Ecclesiastical Courts Commission. The appointment was doubtless owed to Lord Brougham, the new Lord Chancellor, whose reforming views were largely shared by Lushington, a correspondent throughout his life.[13] Lushington was the prime mover behind the commission's proceedings, preparing the questions to be put to witnesses, and drafting most or all of its main report published in 1832.[14] The commissioners proposed a number of sweeping reforms, which Lushington seems to have supported. It first recommended – in a special interim report of 1831 – the abolition of the 'Court' of Delegates.[15] The procedure for issuing *ad hoc* commissions

13 They had both acted as counsel for Queen Caroline, and collaborated in the founding of London University and the Society for the Diffusion of Useful Knowledge.

14 Report of the Commission Appointed to Enquire into the Practice and Jurisdiction of the Ecclesiastical Courts in England and Wales.

15 The practice whereby delegates were appointed to hear ecclesiastical appeals by commission from the Chancery had been introduced in 1534, as a replacement for appeals to the pope and papal delegates: 25 Hen. VIII, c. 19.

to delegates for the hearing of appeals had proved dilatory and expensive, and they were commonly issued to junior practising advocates or persons with insufficient expertise.[16] Parliament responded immediately by transferring the final appellate jurisdiction in English ecclesiastical law to the Privy Council, which was now given a Judicial Committee – a tribunal on which Lushington himself sat from 1838. At the other end of the judicial system, the commission drew attention to the problems arising from the existence of myriad local peculiar jurisdictions, which were inadequately staffed with either judges or counsel. Lushington and the commission favoured the consolidation of all ecclesiastical courts (including abolition even of the Provincial Court of York), the introduction of oral evidence and jury trial,[17] the extension of rights of audience to barristers, and the abolition of the church's criminal and defamation jurisdiction.[18] On the other hand, Lushington urged the retention of the probate and matrimonial jurisdiction, the former in particular because its removal would ruin the proctors and clerks – over 130 men – without any obvious corresponding public benefit.

The future of the profession became a major issue after 1833, when the Real Property Commissioners took the step of recommending the transfer of the testamentary jurisdiction from the church courts to the courts of common law and equity. This was a bombshell which rocked Doctors' Commons to the verge of collapse, since it was 'tantamount to a proposal to annihilate the whole race of Doctors and Proctors at a blow'.[19] Another royal commission was

16 See G. I. O. Duncan, *The High Court of Delegates* (Cambridge, 1971), pp. 28–31.
17 The former was achieved in 1855: below, p. 154.
18 The defamation jurisdiction was abolished in 1856: 18 & 19 Vict., c. 41.
19 Anon., 'The Admiralty and Ecclesiastical Courts', *Law Magazine*, 11 (1834), pp. 447, 448.

appointed, this time taking the Admiralty within its purview, and Lushington testified that the removal of probate jurisdiction would be 'the ruin of the profession'.[20] The new commission reacted by recommending the retention of a civilian profession – albeit opened to bachelors of law,[21] and even masters of arts – on grounds of the national interest in maintaining a body of expertise in international Admiralty law for use in time of war. This argument was put forward by Lushington himself. But, as a contemporary commentator sardonically pointed out, preserving a monopoly on testamentary business to the ecclesiastical courts was a somewhat circuitous way of securing expertise in international law:

> Surely they cannot expect to persuade the public that the study of the law of nations will be neglected unless the doctors have a monopoly of testamentary law conferred upon them, or that the common law and equity bar are unequal to questions involving the construction of treaties or general considerations of expediency. If this be so, how is it that the doctors appear so seldom before the privy council when appeals involving questions of national right are to be discussed?[22]

It was not the most cogent defence of the civilian profession, and from 1833 onwards the civilians were, for good or ill, condemned to extinction.

The recent researches of Professor Waddams have shown that Lushington agonised considerably over his support for these reforms, knowing the effect they would have upon Doctors' Commons. In a surviving draft paper, perhaps prepared for the commissioners, he wrote:

20 Ibid., p. 452.
21 The written English canons required only the LL.B., and the doctorate was still not required for practice in the province of York: above, p. 59.
22 Anon., 'The Admiralty and Ecclesiastical Courts' (1834), at p. 454.

I apprehend that ... with the exception of the profits arising from the office of King's Advocate, the whole gains of the profession amount to scarcely more than one half the income derived by a single eminent counsel at other bars; that the inevitable consequence of this state of things is that the profession must decline, not only in public estimation but in real talent and acquirements, for I must think that there is no present inducement and little future prospect to bring men of ability and industry to the Civil law bar ... I think it is injurious to the public that this state of things should continue ... Notwithstanding the effects upon the bar in Doctors' Commons, not long able (as I believe) even without a change to sustain itself, and which for many reasons I sincerely regret, I must add that the [proposed reforms] appear to me advantages to the public of the greatest value, calculated to render justice more speedy and less expensive, and to destroy a large portion of litigation, the very profitability of which will be removed, the subject-matter no longer existing.[23]

In a letter around the same time to Lord Brougham, Lushington confessed, 'My own opinion is and long has been that the profession must fall; it is vain, I think, to expect that talent will now come in on the bare hope of war'.[24] Rather surprisingly, given that the measure had bipartisan support, the Bill introduced by the Tory government in 1835 to implement the main recommendations of the commission did not pass, and the ecclesiastical courts continued in their unreformed state until the legislation of 1857. Lushington's judicial career, thus prolonged by the

23 Waddams, *Lushington*, pp. 19–20 (punctuation modernised).
24 Ibid., p. 20. The reference to war is to the lucrative prize jurisdiction, which was dormant in times of peace, but had provided
some buoyancy during the Napoleonic wars when Lushington
was first admitted to practice.

failure of his own proposals, was to bring torments of another kind.

In the first place, he was compelled to administer and enforce aspects of ecclesiastical law which he thought deeply unsatisfactory. The most glaring example of his split legal personality is provided by the litigation over church rates, which was made a political issue by Dissenters in the 1830s. Lushington's personal view was that the church could only damage itself by seeking to enforce the payment of church rates against those who refused on grounds of conscience to pay them. He said in 1837 that 'the Church stood by the will of the majority; when the majority was in its favour it reigned paramount, but as the minority who were against it began to increase in number, so it must decline in power, and if it did not give way to their wishes would run a risk of being overturned'.25 Yet, at the very same time that he was campaigning in Parliament for an amendment of the law, he was being called upon as a judge to enforce the law against Dissenters. It was Lushington who found himself in the painful position of having to incarcerate John Thorogood, the 'Church-Rate Martyr', who had arranged to have himself cited in the Consistory Court for the very purpose of putting himself in contempt and thereby gaining publicity. Lushington had little option but to oblige Thorogood by certifying his contempt to the Chancery, where the order was made for his committal. But in doing so he pointed out that there was no law enabling him to release Thorogood unless and until his contempt was purged; he might therefore have found himself in the invidious position of having sent a man to prison for life for failing to pay five shillings and sixpence. The outcome was an Act of Parliament empowering a judge to release a prisoner after six months even if he

25 Speech in the House of Commons, quoted in Waddams, *Lushington*, p. 251.

had not purged his contempt.[26] Lushington continued to be plagued throughout his career by church-rate cases, which constituted the largest single category of suit coming before him as Dean of the Arches. Church rates were not abolished till 1868, the year after his retirement.

As Judge of the Consistory Court, Lushington presided over numerous matrimonial causes. Although he held traditional views on the subjection of wives to their husbands, and on the duty of husbands to control their wives, he was genuinely sympathetic to wronged wives, and in his career at the bar his two most famous clients were Lady Byron and Queen Caroline. He urged Parliament to accord women the same rights to divorce as men, and favoured the introduction of secular judicial divorce on the ground that it might help them to achieve equal access to the law. As a judge, however, he had inherited Lord Stowell's conservative policy towards matrimonial litigation and showed little inclination to modify it. Divorce *a mensa et thoro* was available only in the case of physical danger,[27] and Dr Lushington continued to apply this principle himself, proclaiming that it was no part of the judicial function to interfere in marriages to ensure the personal happiness – as opposed to the safety – of the parties.[28] In a case of divorce *a vinculo*, he declared in the same vein, 'It may be true that ... if the marriage could be set aside it might be productive of happiness and comfort to all parties concerned; but true it also is that I am to decide the question as if no

26 3 & 4 Vict., c. 93; Waddams, *Lushington*, pp. 254–56.

27 *Evans* v. *Evans* (1790) 1 Hag. Con. 35; *Harris* v. *Harris* (1813) 2 Phill. Ecc. 111; 2 Hag. Con. 148; followed by Dr Lushington in the Consistory Court in *Kenrick* v. *Kenrick* (1831) 4 Hagg. Ecc. 114, 129; *Neeld* v. *Neeld* (1831) ibid. 263; *Evans* v. *Evans* (1843) 1 Not. Cas. 570.

28 *Dysart* v. *Dysart* (1844) 1 Rob. Ecc. 106. Lushington's judgment was reversed (on the facts) by the Court of Arches: ibid., p. 470.

such considerations belonged to it ...'[29] The reforms of 1857, when matrimonial causes were removed to a secular court, were not intended to change and in fact did little to change the substance of the law of divorce and separation. Indeed, the bishops continued to oppose equality for wives until the present century, and it was not achieved until 1923.

In the field of probate, Lushington advocated the imposition of formal requirements in order to reduce the amount of tedious, expensive and often unpredictable litigation, and the case was accepted by Parliament in passing the Wills Act 1837. However, as with the Statute of Frauds 1677, which had had a similar object, the introduction of compulsory formalities had the serious side-effect of causing injustice when they had for some reason been omitted or bungled. Lushington found himself on more than one occasion obliged by virtue of his own reforms to render a judgment which he admitted would cause hardship, in order to preserve the greater public interest which he believed would follow from insistence on due form.[30]

Perhaps the most painful of the judicial predicaments in which Dr Lushington found himself were those which did at least belong more naturally to the spiritual jurisdiction. But they were problems for which a court of law, and a judge of Dr Lushington's qualities, were ill suited to resolve. It might even be maintained that the famous series of test cases in which Lushington played such a central part served in the end to weaken the relationship between the church and the law of the land. Nevertheless it is easy to feel sympathy for him as he struggled to impose dispassionate legal logic upon highly contentious religious issues under the fierce scrutiny of the new and increasingly fervent

29 *Ray* v. *Sherwood* (1836) 1 Curt. 173, 192.
30 E.g., *Croker* v. *Hertford* (1844) 4 Moo. P.C. 339; *Hudson* v. *Parker* (1844) 1 Rob. Ecc. 14; Waddams, *Lushington*, pp. 189–93.

opposing factions in the church. Lushington was an old-fashioned churchman, with essentially eighteenth-century tastes in liturgy and ceremonial, and a firm believer in the constitutional position of the established church, preserved (as he saw it) by the sixteenth-century martyrs from the superstitious idolatry of Rome. On the other hand, as a strong liberal he favoured the extension not merely of toleration but of full civil privileges to Dissenters, Roman Catholics and Jews, and he spoke and voted accordingly in Parliament. He also supported the reform embodied in the Marriage Act 1836, which introduced the civil form of marriage, and would indeed have gone further than the legislation by requiring a civil form of marriage in all cases and leaving it to the parties to decide what religious rites they would observe subsequently. His liberal opinions inspired his political career. But was it the task of an ecclesiastical judge to hold the balance impartially between differing interpretations of the Christian faith, or was it to conserve the Church of England as he found it? Should the courts try to ease the growing tensions in the church, or should they adhere steadfastly to the status quo? These had probably not been burning issues in Doctors' Commons when Lushington was first admitted in 1808. But in the Indian summer of that ancient profession, a doctor of law found himself at the centre of dire religious controversy.

The first battle opened in 1849 when the Reverend George Cornelius Gorham brought suit against Henry Phillpotts, Bishop of Exeter,[31] for refusing to institute him to a benefice to which he had been presented by the patron.[32] Gorham was a clergyman of forty years standing, and a former Fellow of Queens' College, Cambridge, but the bishop had taken

31 Not to be confused with the more staid and sensible Henry Philpott, Bishop of Worcester 1860–90, formerly Master of St Catharine's College, Cambridge.
32 Waddams, *Lushington*, pp. 271–80.

exception to him for his allegedly Calvinist leanings. It was
hardly the act of a neutral bishop to subject Gorham to an
extraordinary fifty-hour long interrogation on the doctrine
of baptismal regeneration, a gruelling examination which
the candidate was doubtless intended to fail and therefore
did fail. The Dean of the Arches, Dr Jenner Fust, decided
against Gorham,33 but the decision was reversed by the Privy
Council,34 and Lushington played a major role in the appellate proceedings. The case provoked over 140 pamphlets,
and the legal arguments alone ran to hundreds of pages. It
was perhaps the nearest the Church of England had come
to a heresy trial since the Reformation, and it was upon a
question so subtle and complex that the theology could
hardly be resolved to anyone's satisfaction by a court of
law. The courts indeed struggled to keep the theology at
arm's length, and concentrated on the fairness of the examination and the absence of any specific statement by the
bishop of the points on which Gorham was deemed to be
in error. Lord Langdale, in announcing the resolution of the
Judicial Committee, said that the role of the court was
simply to interpret the Articles of Religion and the Liturgy
according to the same principles of construction as were
applied to all written instruments. The decision nevertheless
prompted a number of Tractarians, including Archdeacon
Manning, to defect to Rome. For both sides, it seemed at
the least inappropriate that such a question should be settled
in the end by a secular body.35

A few years later a controversy of similar gravity was

33 *Gorham* v. *Bishop of Exeter* (1849) 2 Rob. Ecc. 1.
34 *Gorham* v. *Bishop of Exeter* (1850) Br. & Fr. 64; more fully
   reported in E. F. Moore, ed., *The Case of Gorham against the
   Bishop of Exeter* (1852).
35 Lushington had in 1847 drafted a Bill for adding bishops and even
   professors of divinity to the Judicial Committee: Waddams, *Lushington*, p. 279.

begun by the Venerable George Anthony Denison,[36] Archdeacon of Taunton, who as examining chaplain to the
Bishop of Bath and Wells had been requiring ordinands to
indicate their assent to the doctrine that even an unfaithful
or unworthy communicant actually received the Body and
Blood of Christ. This was a theological position then deemed
little short of papistical, and proceedings were commenced
before the archbishop – the bishop being patron of his living
– to deprive Denison under the provisions of the Church
Discipline Act 1840.[37] The archbishop (Sumner) was disin-
clined to sit, and had to be compelled to do so by *mandamus*;
in the event, he is said to have slept in court each day and
– more commendably – to have left the conduct of the
proceedings entirely to Dr Lushington as his chief assessor.
The judgment was that Denison be deprived, though the
Court of Arches restored him, and the Privy Council side-
stepped the issue by holding that the proceedings had been
out of time in the first place.[38] Thus did the courts of law
tackle the vexed question of the Real Presence. Lushington
suffered a good deal of criticism for his part in this decision,
and was accused of allowing personal religious sympathies
to affect his judgment. If the Gorham decision could be said
to represent toleration of diversity in opinions, Lushington's
decision in the Denison case would have made it difficult
for high churchmen to remain in the Church of England.
Gladstone, indeed, wrote that it made 'the cup of disgust
overflow' to recollect that the same set of canons and principles could be used to produce such different results.[39]

36 Ibid., pp. 280–88.
37 3 & 4 Vict., c. 86.
38 *Ditcher* v. *Denison* (1857) 11 Moo. P.C. 324. The decision of the
   Court of Arches is reported in Deane 334. The application for
   mandamus is reported as R. v. *Archbishop of Canterbury* (1856)
   1 E. & B. 546.
39 Passage quoted in Waddams, *Lushington*, pp. 286–87.

Lushington's defence was that in Gorham's case the charges
of unsoundness were too imprecise to be made out, whereas
in Denison's case the doctrine which he preached was un-
ambiguously contrary to the Articles.

Before this case had been finally determined, the more
mundane but equally explosive question of ornament had
been raised by the case of St Barnabas, Pimlico.[40] The church
had been built in 1850 and decorated in the Gothic style
pioneered by Pugin and now regarded as characteristic of
Victorian churches. So far in fact has the Victorian Gothic
fashion come to control our image of church taste that it is
easy to forget what a great and controversial change the
introduction of neo-medieval ornament and colour wrought
at the time. Of course, there was nothing scandalous or
novel about medieval styles of church architecture as such,
and no conceivable objection to emulating the Early English
style of building. But the medieval churches of Lushington's
youth had plain interiors and sparse decoration, without
crucifixes, changing liturgical colours or large altar candle-
sticks. So shocking, in the 1850s, was the appearance of the
new church in Pimlico that legal proceedings were commenced to outlaw the stone altar, the credence table, the
cross and candles, and the use of liturgical colours. The case
came before Dr Lushington as Judge of the Consistory
Court, and he tried again to defuse the situation by declaring
that the matter required 'a dry and tedious inquiry into
doubtful propositions of positive law'.[41] He nevertheless did
not contrive, and perhaps did not believe it necessary, to
preserve an open mind as between the status quo and the

40 Ibid., pp. 288–97.
41 *Westerton* v. *Liddell* (1855), reported in a separate volume edited
by A. F. Bayford; (1857) Br. & Fr. 117 (P. C.). Note also *Flamank*
v. *Simpson* (1866) L. R. 1 Ad. & Ecc. 276 (prosecution for using
candles on the communion table when not needed for illumination).

new Roman tendency which had already led a hundred clergymen to secede from the Church of England and which threatened to create splinter parishes. He referred in his judgment to the 'just abhorrence' felt at any usage which had 'the remotest leaning to the Church of Rome', whose usages were characterised by 'a meretricious display of fantastic and unnecessary ornament'. The ornaments were insignificant in themselves, but by association they amounted to 'a servile imitation of the Church of Rome' and were therefore dangerous. 'Chastity and simplicity are not at variance with grandeur and beauty; but they are not reconcilable with jewels, lace, variegated cloths, and embroidery.' All that is missing from the judgment is a reference to the Whore of Babylon.[42] It brought still more obloquy on Lushington, who was upheld by the Court of Arches but reversed by the Privy Council on every point except that concerning the stone altar. The dispute was the first in a long series of well-known cases on ornament which continued until the end of the century, and which cumulatively rejected Lushington's position. One result, as he predicted, was the creation of parishes with what were then seen as Roman tendencies, parishes which by experimenting with forgotten usages drove away parishioners wishing to follow more familiar ways; but this was less open to objection in Pimlico than in a remote country village.

The next legal controversy to arise, in 1859, concerned the practice of confession and absolution, which had recently been reintroduced by some high church priests.[43] A complaint had been laid by two women against the Reverend Alfred Poole, Stipendiary Curate of the same church of St Barnabas, Pimlico, for asking them lewd questions during confession, and the Bishop of London had revoked his

42 Waddams, *Lushington*, p. 293.
43 Ibid., pp. 297–302.

licence. Archbishop Sumner tried to dispose of the case by correspondence, but was again compelled by *mandamus* to provide a formal hearing. Lushington sat as assessor and conducted the proceedings. He was now aged seventy-seven, and both he and the archbishop – two years his senior – fought a desperate struggle against slumber during the arguments. The complainants' submission was not that confession and absolution were illegal, but that young priests ought not to subject women to disgusting and improper questions about their sexual conduct.44 There was some reticence about discussing the exact nature of the questions, and the accusations against Poole do not seem to have been any more precise than those against Gorham, but Dr Lushington nevertheless decided against him. In this case the Privy Council declined jurisdiction to hear an appeal.45

As if all these problems were not enough, the 1860s brought a great debate over the authority of the Bible.46 In the highly controversial *Essays and Reviews* (1860) it was daringly claimed that the Bible could be subjected to textual criticism on the basis that not everything which it contained was literally true or even divinely inspired. This was an assertion quite unacceptable to the high church, which was still smarting from Darwin's blasphemous scientific questioning of the Book of Genesis. Two of the essayists – the Reverend Dr Rowland Williams, Vicar of Broad Chalk, and the Reverend Henry Bristow Wilson, Vicar of Great Staughton – were cited before the consistory courts for what the law reports refer

44 In *R. v. Hicklin* (1868) L.R. 3 Q.B. 360, some language in a confessional manual was actually held to be criminally obscene.
45 *Poole v. Bishop of London* (1861) 14 Moo. P. C. 262. The decision at first instance is reported in *The Times* (references in Waddams, *Lushington*).
46 Waddams, *Lushington*, pp. 310–46.

to as 'heresy',47 and their cases were removed into the Court of Arches. Once more Lushington emphasised that his court was not a court of divinity but of ecclesiastical law, though he acknowledged that no court could be asked to decide a more important question than 'what was sufficient for the salvation of the human race'. According to Article VI, 'Holy Scripture containeth all things necessary to salvation ...', but nowhere in the Articles is it stated that everything in Holy Scripture is to be believed literally or that every word was written down by direct divine interposition. Lushington nevertheless decided that the two clergymen should be deprived. The principal charge against Dr Williams was that he had declared the Bible to be an 'expression of devout reason', which was held to be inconsistent with the necessary implication of the expression 'God's word written' in Article XX. Mr Wilson was deprived principally for expressing the hope that even the wicked would find 'refuge in the bosom of the Universal Parent', a sentiment which Lushington considered inconsistent with the mention of everlasting fire in the Athanasian Creed. Both decisions were reversed by the Privy Council. In the case of Dr Williams, it was held that his expressions did not on a reasonable construction support a criminal charge of maintaining that the Bible was not the word of God. As to Mr Wilson, although the board did not doubt that God might condemn the wicked to eternal misery, they could find nothing in the formularies to render it illegal for a clergyman to express the hope that God might ultimately grant them pardon.48 Lushington's decision on the

---

47 The formal charge was of setting forth doctrines contrary to the doctrines of the Church of England contained in the Articles of Religion, the Book of Common Prayer and the Formularies.

48 *Bishop of Salisbury* v. *Williams*; *Fendall* v. *Wilson* (1863) 2 Moo. P. C. (N. S.) 375. The decision at first instance is reported in 1 New Rep. 196 (not in the *English Reports*), and in a separate volume printed in 1862.

authority of Scripture is particularly difficult to follow, since he had dismissed some of the charges against Dr Wilson – for instance, that relating to the historical truth of the Flood – on the ground that parts of the Bible were more historical and less sacred than others, that the text must contain copying errors and mistranslations, and also that some passages were allegories not meant to be taken as literal truth. For these latter propositions, which were not the subject of appeal, Lushington's judgment was praised as liberal; but it was said afterwards by counsel that neither party was satisfied by the final result. Lord Westbury L.C. for his part earned the jocular rebuke that he had 'dismissed hell with costs and taken away from orthodox members of the Church of England their last hope of everlasting damnation'.[49]

Whether it was right for questions of such a character to be resolved by lawyers, with appeal to such an essentially secular body as the Judicial Committee of the Privy Council, was a matter of legitimate debate and was a major factor in the decision of clergymen such as Manning to remove themselves to a church in which the ultimate authority was spiritual. But this was not Lushington's fault, and he always disclaimed jurisdiction over purely theological questions. The proper toleration which the law accorded to those of diverse religious persuasions, and which Lushington actively supported in Parliament, could not be extended by an English court to ministers of the Church of England. The clergy of the established church were by law bound to maintain the doctrine and worship of the church as settled in the sixteenth century. This was a matter of law rather than of freedom of religion, since no one was compelled to be a Church of England priest, and Dr Lushington maintained that such questions could and ought to be decided on purely

49 J. B. Atlay, *The Victorian Chancellors* (1908), ii, p. 264, quoted in Waddams, *Lushington*, p. 331.

legal grounds, by construing the relevant articles and formularies of faith, and avoiding extrinsic theological or
political issues. It is, however, still perhaps an open question
how far he succeeded in keeping the law insulated from the
realms of theological controversy, and whether the Victorian
church benefited from having these burning issues filtered
through courts of law dominated (in the Privy Council) by
politicians.

At the same time as these great debates were placing Dr
Lushington and his brother civilians briefly at the centre of
the national stage, they were having to make agonising
decisions of a more domestic nature concerning their own
separation and divorce. Upon the passage of the 1857 legislation, which permitted serjeants and barristers at law to
appear in the new probate and divorce courts,[50] it was
obvious that the end had now come for the profession of
civilian advocates. A contemporary described the doctors at
this time as 'moving in a kind of ancient twilight',[51] which
was no doubt widely expected to give way presently to the
total darkness of final extermination. Provision was made
in the Court of Probate Act 1857 for the College of Doctors
of Law to surrender their charter to the Crown, whereupon
the corporation would be dissolved and all the real and
personal estate would belong to the members in equal shares
as tenants in common for their own use.[52] After a rearguard
action to prevent it,[53] the property – including the magnificent library – was sold, and the proceeds shared among
the members, excepting the colours of the civilian volunteer

---

50 Court of Probate Act 1857, 20 & 21 Vict., c. 77; Matrimonial
   Causes Act 1857, 20 & 21 Vict., c. 85.
51 'The Inns of Court', *Illustrated London News* (4 April 1857),
   p. 315, quoting a 'high legal authority'.
52 20 & 21 Vict., c. 77, s. 117.
53 Some papers relating to these events, preserved by Dr Lee, are in
   Lambeth Palace, MS 1560.

corps, which were presented to the Inner Temple.54 But the civilians' divorce was *a mensa et thoro* and not *a vinculo*, for the charter was not in the event surrendered, and the corporation was not therefore dissolved under the terms of section 117. The last meeting of the college was held on 10 July 1865, when Dr Lushington (as Dean of the Arches) was still president. His prediction of professional extinction had come to pass, albeit thirty eventful years later than he had anticipated.

Stephen Lushington D.C.L. (1778–1873), later Judge of the Court of Adniralty and Dean of Arches, drawn in 1824. Stipple engraving by W. Holl after a pencil drawing by A. Wivell, 20 April 1824.

From a print in the possession of the author

54 The Military Association was formed in 1798 to protect the English civil lawyers against Napoleon.

15

Sir Robert Phillimore

HE last great civilian author from Doctors' Commons, Sir Robert Phillimore, was born to the law.[1] His father Joseph Phillimore (1775–1855), the son of a country vicar, had been admitted as an advocate in 1804.[2] Old Dr Phillimore had two sons. The elder, John George Phillimore (1808–65), was called to the Bar, took silk, and became a Bencher of Lincoln's Inn in 1851; but he bore the civilian gene, and wrote several books and tracts on Roman and canon law.[3] Indeed, he espoused the eccentric view – distinctly eccentric for a practising silk – that many of the contemporary defects in English law were due to neglect of the study of Roman law.[4] The

---

1 There is a brief life by Lord Sumner in *DNB*, xii, pp. 1073–74. See also E. Manson, *The Builders of our Law during the Reign of Queen Victoria* (1895), pp. 163–68; Holdsworth, *History of English Law*, xvi, pp. 146–50. Several boxes of his draft papers and offprints are preserved at Christ Church, Oxford, where he was a Student.

2 See the biographical note by J. M. Rigg in *DNB*, xv, p. 1071. The family had originally spelt its name Fynamore, or Phinimore, and changed to the later spelling in the seventeenth century: *Burke's Peerage and Baronetage* (105th edn, 1980), pp. 2114–16.

3 J. G. Phillimore, *Introduction to the Study and History of Roman Law* (1848); idem, 'Influence of the Canon Law' (in *Oxford Essays*, 1858); idem, *Private Law among the Romans from the Pandects* (1863). He also delivered a 'reading' on canon law in the Middle Temple in 1851. See also *DNB*, xv, p. 1071 (biography by J. M. Rigg).

4 Holdsworth, *History of English Law*, xv, p. 360. See J. G. Phillimore, *Principles and Maxims of Jurisprudence* (1856), which is

second son, Robert Joseph (1810–85), followed his father to
Westminster School and Christ Church and was admitted
to Doctors' Commons in 1839. An early interest in politics
was revealed in a pamphlet of 1837, in which he defended
the constitutional monarchy against the so-called 'democratic' – meaning republican – notions which had been
cultivated in radical circles since the Reform Act.5 His dislike
of extremes led him to the middle ground, and in 1852 he
was actually elected to the Commons as a 'Liberal-Conser-
vative'. In his Coventry election manifesto of 1857, preserved
in Christ Church, he declared himself 'opposed to all violent
and organic changes in the framework of our Constitution',
yet in favour of wise reforms, and concluded that he was
both Conservative and Liberal. On this occasion his admir-
able political centrality did not secure him a seat; he never
returned to Parliament, and he is not remembered as a pol-
itician, though he became a long-standing friend and
correspondent of Gladstone,6 who conferred a baronetcy
upon him in 1881. After leaving the Commons he continued
to be active in public life, and served on numerous royal
commissions: on the Royal Courts of Justice (1859), Judicature (1867), Ritual (1867), Naturalisation (1868)
and Neutrality (1868). His professional interest in international law, developed as a law officer during the American
Civil War, and reflected in an important treatise,7 led him
in 1875 to chair the Alberico Gentili Committee,8 and in

---

primarily an exercise in comparative law.

5 R. Phillimore, *The Constitution as it is or Democracy?* (1837).

6 Mrs Gladstone was godmother to Sir Robert's eldest daughter
Catherine.

7 R. Phillimore, *Commentaries upon International Law* (1854–61),
four volumes. There were three editions.

8 The principal purposes were to erect a memorial tablet in St
Helen's, Bishopsgate, and to print a new edition of *De jure belli
et pacis*: papers in Christ Church.

Demolition of Doctors' Commons, showing the north side of the quadrangle with the entrance from Knightrider Street. Woodcut by W. J. Palmer from *Illustrated London News*, 4 May 1867, p. 440.

1879 to become President of the Association for the Reformation and Codification of the Law of Nations.9

Phillimore received the appointment of Admiralty Advocate in 1855 and of Queen's Advocate-General in 1862,10 and was the last major civilian judge, becoming the final holder of the ancient office of Judge of the Admiralty, and serving as Dean of the Arches from 1867. He also served as Judge of the Cinque Ports, an office his father had held before him, from 1855 to 1875. The office of Dean of Arches by itself was more a professional honour than a position of

9 See *International Law: Inaugural Lecture Delivered by Sir Robert Phillimore* [to the Association] (1879).
10 He was succeeded as Queen's Advocate by Sir Travers Twiss, who was not replaced upon his resignation in 1872; the office has been in abeyance since then. The last Admiralty Advocate was Dr Deane (following Twiss).

profit, and Phillimore made a public complaint in 1872 that his remuneration in that office was insufficient to cover his expenses. He had accepted the office because of the 'crisis' caused by the resignation of Dr Lushington, but the latter had clung to the lucrative office of Master of the Faculties, traditionally the principal source of remuneration for the Dean of Arches.[11] Phillimore obtained the latter office on Lushington's death in 1873, but his position was about to be transformed by the Judicature Acts. The Judge of the Admiralty became automatically a judge of the new High Court in 1875, but by virtue of section 11 of the Judicature Act 1873 he would have retained his former rank and salary, which was lower than that of other puisne judges. Before the first Act came into force, the Judicature Act 1875 provided that 'the existing Judge of the High Court of Admiralty' (meaning Phillimore) should have the same rank, salary and pension as if he had been newly appointed to the High Court, provided that he resigned all offices of emolument except the office of Judge of the Admiralty.[12] Phillimore thereupon resigned the office of Dean of Arches and Master of the Faculties, and served as a High Court judge in the Probate, Divorce and Admiralty Division until his retirement in 1883,[13] sitting chiefly – as it seems from the *Law Reports* – in Admiralty.[14] He was the only member

11 R. Phillimore, *Clergy Discipline: A Letter to His Grace the Archbishop of Canterbury from Sir R[ober]t Phillimore* (1872), p. 8. See also S. M. Waddams, *Law, Politics and the Church of England: The Career of Stephen Lushington, 1782–1873* (Cambridge, 1992), p. 9.

12 Supreme Court of Judicature Act 1873 (36 & 37 Vict., c. 66), ss. 5, 11; Supreme Court of Judicature Act 1875 (38 & 39 Vict., c. 77), s. 8.

13 J. Sainty, *The Judges of England, 1272–1990*, Selden Society, Supplementary Series, 10 (1993), p. 220.

14 Lord Penzance, President of the Probate, Divorce and Admiralty Division, had succeeded Phillimore as Dean of Arches in 1875. He was not a civilian.

Sir Robert Joseph Phillimore D.C.L. (1811–85), Queen's Advocate 1862-67, Dean of Arches 1867–75, later a Justice of the High Court. Photograph by the London Stereoscopic Company, *c.* 1867.

From a photograph in the possession of the author

of Doctors' Commons ever appointed to the High Court,[15] though he was qualified in the traditional way as a Queen's Counsel and Bencher of the Middle Temple (1858).[16]

Phillimore had joined Doctors' Commons, perhaps out of filial piety, at a time when it was already doomed. As early as 1843, when a young advocate, he had published an impassioned plea for the retention of the advocates' monopoly of audience as it faced a renewed threat.[17] To the conservative side of his disposition, it was an affront that an institution which had survived for so many centuries should be threatened when there were no serious complaints against it. It was an age, he lamented, in which every existing institution was called upon to show cause why it should not be destroyed, whereas in the past the burden of proof had been on those advocating reform. In this age, he observed, 'every possessor of a few current phrases, easily learnt and glibly enunciated, and every retailer of a few resuscitated fallacies (innocently believed to be new truths), entertains no doubt as to his full competency to criticise and condemn what the wise and learned of former times have cherished and upheld'. Admission as an advocate required a longer

---

15 It is notable that none of the judges of the statutory probate and divorce courts between 1858 and 1875 had been civilians.

16 His manuscript reading in the Middle Temple (1861) is at Christ Church. It was said to have been a revival of readings there, albeit in the form of a simple lecture: J. B. Williamson, *The Middle Temple Bench Book* (1937), p. 227. However, his elder brother had given a reading in 1851: above, p. 147 n. 3.

17 R. Phillimore, *The Study of the Civil and Canon Law Considered in its Relation to the State, the Church, and the Universities, and its Connection with the College of Advocates* (1843). A similar discourse was printed as *The Practice and Courts of Ecclesiastical Law ... in a Letter to The Rt Hon. W. E. Gladstone* (1848), responding to charges made in the Commons by Mr E. Pleydell-Bouverie. See also *Speech of Robert Phillimore, Esq., M.P., in the House of Commons, Tuesday, March 1, 1853 on the Motion of Mr Collier* (1853), extracted from Hansard.

period after the first degree than reading for the Bar, a period in which aspiring advocates could acquire a broader knowledge of history and foreign law than barristers would normally think appropriate. 'The Bar,' he lamented, 'has not escaped the predominant vice, which unhappily characterizes our times, a feverish haste to grow rich, at the expense of bodily health, of general knowledge, and of all due and equal cultivation of the mental faculties, while the anxiety to practise before every Court and in every kind of law, tends to substitute a specious smattering in all, for real proficiency in any single branch of jurisprudence.' Quite apart from the special qualifications of the doctors, and their expertise in ecclesiastical and international law, there was the matter of justice: it was no more just to deprive the doctors of their ancient rights than it was to deprive the serjeants, whose monopoly in the Common Pleas had recently been upheld by the judges against the illegal warrant of 1834.[18] That last argument was ill-judged and was soon answered, since Parliament showed no concern for historical titles. The serjeants' monopoly – under constant attack from Lord Brougham – was abolished by an Act of Parliament rushed through in the Long Vacation of 1846.[19] Specialist Bars were no longer acceptable to the powers that be.

Phillimore objected in the same pamphlet to the modern practice of appointing diocesan chancellors who were not doctors of law, despite the statute of 1545 which required that lay chancellors should have the doctorate.[20] The civilian,

---

18 J. Manning, *Serviens ad legem* (1840) (in the Privy Council); *Re the Serjeants at Law* (1839) 6 Bing. N. C. 235 (in the Common Pleas); J. H. Baker, *The Order of Serjeants at Law*, Selden Society, Supplementary Series, 5 (1984), pp. 118–22.

19 Practitioners in Common Pleas Act 1846, 9 & 10 Vict., c. 54; Baker, *Serjeants at Law*, p. 122.

20 Ecclesiastical Jurisdiction Act 1545, 37 Hen. VIII, c. 17 (by virtue of the words 'so that they be Doctors of the Civil Law'); this proviso applied only to laymen. The statute was repealed in 1863.

'being both necessarily versed in this law, and necessarily being a member of the Church of England,[21] combines that admixture of clerical and secular learning which has been wisely held peculiarly to qualify him for the judge, assessor or adviser of the bishop'. This was, of course, another lost cause. The following year Phillimore mounted a defence of the ecclesiastical courts. Their proceedings were less adversarial than trials by jury, and more suited to family disputes. For instance, written evidence, though open to some objections, could sometimes be more reliable than oral testimony given in the heat of a trial.[22] This opinion, as we have seen, was rejected by Dr Lushington, and it was Lushington who prevailed.[23] Dr Phillimore himself came to accept that oral evidence was appropriate in some cases, and introduced a Bill in 1855 to permit viva voce testimony to be given in ecclesiastical courts; he later took some pride in the 'almost total change which the working of this little Statute has produced in the whole procedure of the Courts'.[24] The following year, he was responsible for the Act which abolished the defamation jurisdiction of the church courts.[25]

21 Only a doctorate from Oxford or Cambridge was by this time acceptable.
22 R. Phillimore, *Thoughts on the Law of Divorce in England* (1844), pp. 40–41, cited in Waddams, *Lushington*, p. 14. In idem, *The Practice and Courts of Ecclesiastical Law* (1848), pp. 53–59, he pointed out that the popularity of trial by judge alone had been proved by the free choice of litigants using the new County Courts. He also argued (ibid., pp. 50–51) that detailed positions and articles rendered a party less open to surprise than common-law pleadings.
23 See above, p. 130.
24 R. Phillimore, *Clergy Discipline: A Letter to His Grace the Archbishop of Canterbury from Sir R[obert] Phillimore* (1872), p. 6. The bill was enacted as the Ecclesiastical Courts Act 1855, 17 & 18 Vict., c. 47.
25 Suits for Defamation in Ecclesiastical Courts Act 1856, 18 & 19 Vict., c. 41.

Phillimore is best remembered by lawyers today for his monumental *Ecclesiastical Law of the Church of England* (1873), which contains no less than 2466 pages including the preliminaries and index. He had apparently conceived the idea as a result of his labours as the last editor of Burn's *Ecclesiastical Law* (1842).[26] Although he had introduced various alterations in that edition,[27] Phillimore concluded that Burn's alphabetical arrangement was 'fatal to any attempt to produce the law in the form of a system arranged according to the principles of a science'.[28] His new scheme was certainly more systematic, and yet the book could better be characterised as a typical Victorian practitioner's textbook than a work of intellectual coherence. The historical statements in the treatise were often based on modern judgments in the courts rather than a first-hand assessment of the original evidence, an approach which would soon be condemned for ever by Maitland. But Phillimore belonged to the old school, and was not in any case writing history for its own sake. He evidently saw the book as a compilation for practical use rather than as the historical or jurisprudential monograph which it might have been in the hands of a Maitland. No doubt this is why Maitland did not see fit to criticise or notice it; unlike the works of Twiss or Stubbs, it could not be mistaken for serious historical scholarship.

Phillimore's *Ecclesiastical Law* was divided into ten sections: (1) an introduction dealing with the church and its law; (2) the orders and offices of the church, including benefices and advowsons; (3) 'The church in relation to the general life of the Members', meaning the sacraments and liturgy

---

26 See above, pp. 121–22. Phillimore had also written, in the interim, *The Law of Domicil* (1847); *Practice of Ecclesiastical and Civil Law* (1848).

27 See above, p. 122.

28 R. Phillimore, *Ecclesiastical Law of the Church of England* (1873), preface, p. v.

(including a transcript of Queen Victoria's coronation service); (4) discipline, including the procedure of the church courts; (5) the property of the church, including tithes; (6) fabric, including the duties of churchwardens; (7) councils of the church, including Convocation; (8) charities and education, including the universities; (9) 'church extension', dealing with augmentations, Queen Anne's Bounty and related topics; and (10) the Church of England in relation to other churches (meaning the churches of the Anglican communion throughout the world). The author was uncertain whether to include the universities and colleges in his eighth section, since recent legislation had removed so much of their ecclesiastical character; another consequence of the changes, he thought, had been 'to reduce the colleges to somewhat of their old position as societies in, but not constituent parts of, the university'.29 The book avowedly incorporated a good deal of Burn, and it followed the same abridgmental style in listing more or less unconnected propositions with lavish quotations from judgments and other authorities. Like its precursors, its principal value lay, and – for those seeking the older authorities – still lies, in its comprehensiveness as a collection of materials. Most of its constituent sources were in print, though occasional use was made of manuscript sources: for instance, an opinion of Dr Scott (later Lord Stowell) in 1809, that a vestry could lawfully by a majority vote authorise payment of an organist;30 and that of Dr French Lawrence in 1806 that a minister could not refuse to

---

29 Ibid., p. 1991 (and pp. 2000–1). This opinion was ignored by the University Commissioners in 1993, who decided without any sound reason that the colleges at Oxford and Cambridge were 'constituent colleges' of those universities for the purposes of the Education Reform Act 1988 (c. 40).

30 Phillimore, *Ecclesiastical Law*, pp. 928–29. Nevertheless, he cited authorities showing that an organ was not necessary in a parish church.

baptise the child of a Dissenter on the grounds that the child would be brought up to dissent from the principles of the Church of England.[31]

Notwithstanding the massive proportions of the treatise, Phillimore's principal contributions to ecclesiastical juris-prudence (like Lushington's) were his judgments as Dean of Arches, which often dealt in minute detail with the historical authorities. Like Dr Lushington, he was obliged to wrestle with some highly contentious disputes concerning ornament and ritual, but he did so in a manner calculated to heal differences. Not that he had any sympathy with Rome. Phillimore adhered to the orthodox view of the Church of England as the true catholic church, descended directly from the primitive church, with independent rights which had been recognised in the middle ages – the *ecclesia anglicana* of Magna Carta (1215).[32] The schism between the Eastern and Western Churches was attributable to 'the arrogance, ambition and un-catholic conduct of Rome', and further divisions had been 'aggravated by the new dogmas which Rome has recently promulgated, founded upon a new theory of development which shakes the stability of all Christian faith'. The Vatican Council of 1870, indeed, was in Philli-more's view of dubious canonical validity, and its doctrine of papal infallibility 'at variance with all sound catholic teaching and principle'.[33] Rome had, in short, left the cath-olic church and set up on its own. But that did not mean that practices current before the Reformation were wrong

31 Ibid., pp. 647–48. Dr Lawrence pointed out that ministers were obliged to baptise papists' children under the Presentation to Benefices Act 1605, 3 Jac. I, c. 5, s. 14 (repealed in 1843).

32 In addition to the next work cited, see also his judgment in *Martin v. Mackonochie* (1868) L. R. 2 A. & E. 116, at pp. 150–74 (Court of Arches).

33 Phillimore, *Ecclesiastical Law*, pp. 2, 1922.

or unlawful merely because they had been discontinued in England; there was a shared catholic inheritance.

Phillimore was engaged in most of the important cases on ritual and ornament in the 1850s and 1860s,34 and in 1866 advised the English Church Union on the lawfulness of the recent revival of 'some ancient Ecclesiastical Usages'.35 He held in a case of 1870 that:

> It is a mistake in law, as well as in history, to conceive that the position of the Church of England with respect to the Roman Church can be ascertained by citations of the violent vituperations to be found during the heat of religious conflict in the writings of some extreme reformers – some of whom, upon examination, will be found to be just as hostile to the present doctrines and ceremonies of England as they were at that time to those of Rome.36

In deciding on the lawfulness of ceremonies, it was necessary to distinguish between those which were immutable and 'those which it is competent to mould according to the varying necessities and exigencies of each particular church'.37 This distinction, as he said in the same case, 'divested the issue of the case before me of that importance which has been, not unnaturally, perhaps, ascribed to it by the excited

34 E.g., *Liddell v. Westerton* (1856), printed as *Argument of Robert Phillimore D.C.L. in the Court of Arches in the Matter of the Ornaments of St Paul and St Barnabas, Knightsbridge* (1856); *Speech of Robert Phillimore, D.C.L., Q.C., in the Case of The Office of the Judge Promoted by the Bishop of Salisbury against Williams* (1862).

35 G. H. Brooks, *Ritual Ornaments and Usages: A Case Submitted on Behalf of the English Church Union; with the Opinions of Her Majesty's Advocate (Sir R. Phillimore, Q.C.); Sir Fitzroy Kelly, Q.C. ...* (1866), which was a response to *The Ornaments of the Minister* (1866).

36 *Elphinstone v. Purchas* (1870) L.R.3 A.&E. 66, at p. 80.

37 *Martin v. Mackonochie* (1868) L.R.2 A.& E. 116, at p. 136.

feelings of both parties'.[38] In assessing mutable usages, when they were not expressly prohibited by English authorities, 'the true criterion is conformity with primitive and catholic use, and not antagonism to Rome'.[39] Mere disuse was not a fatal objection, since some of the catholic usages of the early church which had become disused were perfectly lawful, but it was necessary to distinguish truly catholic usages from 'the novelties and additions which the Curia of Rome had from time to time imposed upon its subjects'.[40] Phillimore, here as elsewhere, was careful to distinguish between the innovations of the Roman 'Curia' – preferring not to refer to the Roman Church as a distinct entity – and the true catholic usages of the Church of England, which were based on ancient tradition. He was less careful about defining the chronological turning point, if there was one, when Rome began to break away from the catholic tradition. Clearly it had done so since the Council of Trent; but to some extent it had done so prior to the sixteenth century, for otherwise the Reformation would have been unnecessary. In his treatise, he indicates that he considered the problems to have begun at least as far back as the Lateran Council of 1215 – 'untruly styled the twelfth general or oecumenical council' – which introduced the novel doctrine of transubstantiation.[41]

In approaching the contentious theological issues which came before him as a judge, Phillimore was slightly more liberal than the Privy Council towards practices then widely perceived as Roman, and as a consequence he was frequently reversed. He took the view that 'The basis of the religious establishment in this realm was, I am satisfied, intended by the constitution and the law to be broad, and not narrow', and

38 Ibid., p. 146.
39 Ibid., pp. 149, 174 (put as a proposition, which he later accepts).
40 *Elphinstone* v. *Purchas* (1870) L. R. 3 A. & E. 66, at p. 79.
41 Phillimore, *Ecclesiastical Law*, at p. 676.

that 'within its walls there is room, if they could cease from litigation' for both the Tractarian and the traditional wings of the Church of England.42 Nevertheless, his concept of a broad church, in the context of liturgy, would be thought somewhat narrow today. The first major test came in *Martin* v. *Mackonochie* (1868), in which he held unlawful the elevation of the consecrated elements, the use of incense as a ceremony associated solely with Holy Communion, and the practice of adding water to the wine during the consecration, because these all amounted to new and unauthorised ceremonies; but in the same case he held it not to be a criminal offence for the priest to indulge in excessive kneeling or prostration, for lighted candles to be placed on the altar though not needed for illumination, or for the wine to be mingled with water before the Communion service. On all these three last points, though with some doubts as to the last, he was reversed by the Privy Council,43 but the parties dragged the dispute on for another fifteen years until Mackonochie was finally deprived for contempt.44 In the second of the Mackonochie cases, Phillimore held it unlawful to sing the *Agnus Dei* between the consecration and the reception of the Communion, and for the priest to make the sign of the cross in the air to the congregation.45 He acknowledged and followed the Privy Council decision of 1868 as to candles and incense in a similar case in 1870.46 But in the same year Phillimore reiterated his doctrine as to the mingling of water and wine *before* the consecration, and held in the same case that it was lawful for the priest to wear a chasuble, tunic and alb, for wafer

42 *Martin* v. *Mackonochie* (1868) L. R. 2 A. & E. 116, at p. 245.
43 *Martin* v. *Mackonochie* (1868) L. R. 2 P. C. 365.
44 *Mackonochie* v. *Lord Penzance* (1881) 6 App. Cas. 424; *Martin* v. *Mackonochie* (No. 3) (1882) 7 P. D. 94 (Privy Council); (1883) 8 P. D. 191 (Court of Arches).
45 *Martin* v. *Mackonochie* (No. 2) (1874) L. R. 4 A. & E. 279 (Court of Arches).
46 *Sumner* v. *Wix* (1870) L. R. 3 A. & E. 58 (Court of Arches).

bread to be used for Communion, and for the priest to stand with his back to the congregation during the consecration. On all these points, he was again reversed by the Privy Council. The only concession to 'Roman' tendencies which the Privy Council accepted was that it was not *necessarily* unlawful for a priest to wear, or at least to carry, a biretta.[47]

Also in the year 1870, Phillimore was asked to decide a case concerning the doctrine of transubstantiation. A clergyman had been prosecuted for heresy, and the essential question concerned the nature of the 'real' or objective presence in the consecrated elements. After reviewing a mass of historical authorities, including a text set out in the *Law Reports* in Greek, Phillimore decided that it was lawful to assert a real presence, which could be understood in a mystic or spiritual sense, and to speak of the Communion as a sacrifice; but that it was unlawful to teach that there was a visible presence of Our Lord at the time of celebration, or to indulge in a supersititious adoration of the elements.[48]

In 1874 Phillimore reversed a judgment of the Bishop of Exeter, given on the advice of Keating J. as assessor, that the new reredos with images in Exeter Cathedral was illegal; in justification of his more liberal approach, he was able to cite an unreported sentence of the Court of Arches in 1684.[49] But he remained conservative with respect to the legal status of Hell, which was raised in a novel manner in 1875:[50] could

---

47 *Elphinstone* v. *Purchas* (1870) L. R. 3 A. & E. 66; continued as *Hebbert* v. *Purchas*, L. R. 3 P. C. 605; 19 W. R. 898. The dispute over these matters continued to rage when Lord Penzance was Dean of Arches: see *Ridsdale* v. *Clifton* (1877) 2 P. D. 276; *Combe* v. *Edwards* (1877) 2 P. D. 354.

48 *Sheppard* v. *Bennett* (1870) L. R. 3 A. & E. 167. A preliminary issue is reported at (1868) L. R. 2 A. & E. 335.

49 *Boyd* v. *Phillpotts* (1874) L. R. 4 A. & E. 297, citing *Cocke* v. *Tallants* (1684) from the records of the Arches.

50 The previous leading case on Hell was *Fendall* v. *Wilson* (1863) 2 Moo. P. C. (N. S.) 375; above, p. 142.

a parish priest deny Communion to someone who had denied the doctrine of eternal punishment, as being a heretic? Phillimore decided that such a person was an 'evil liver' and could lawfully be turned away, but the Privy Council reversed the decision on the ground that evil living referred to moral rather than theological delinquency.[51]

Not all decisions of the Court of Arches during Phillimore's deanship were as contentious as these, though some interesting legal issues of different kinds were brought before him. For example, in 1868, thirty years before Parliament extended the principle to ordinary criminal cases, Phillimore held that as a consequence of the Evidence Act 1851 a defendant in a criminal suit under the Church Discipline Act 1840 was both competent and compellable to give evidence.[52] And in 1873 it was held that solicitors were not entitled to practise in the Court of Arches unless they were also proctors. Phillimore stated obiter in this case that in so far as barristers had been allowed to argue in the court it was out of courtesy rather than as of right.[53] If he was correct on this latter point, it may still be the case that only doctors of law have a *right* of audience in the Court of Arches, barristers being admitted out of necessity for want of practising doctors.

Among the less portentous cases which came before him, Sir Robert had to consider in 1875 who was entitled to the style 'Reverend'. He pointed out that the style had formerly been used for laymen and even women, and that it could not logically be regarded as confined to clergymen of a particular denomination; it was nevertheless proper for a faculty to be

---

51 *Jenkins* v. *Cook* (1875) L. R. 4 Adm. & Ecc. 463; 1 P. D. 80.
52 *Bishop of Norwich* v. *Pearse* (1868) L. R. 2 A. & E. 281. This was because the exception in the Evidence Act (14 & 15 Vict., c. 99) referring to criminal cases was not drawn widely enough to include such proceedings.
53 *Burch* v. *Reid* (1873) L. R. 4 A. & E. 112; followed by Lord Penzance in *Crisp* v. *Martin* (1876) 1 P. D. 302.

refused where it was proposed to be used in a monumental inscription to describe a Wesleyan minister.54 The decision as to the refusal was reversed by the Privy Council, which nevertheless confirmed Phillimore's principal holding: the style 'Reverend' is not a title but merely a complimentary epithet.55 It follows, of course, that it is a piece of conceit for a clergyman to use the style in describing himself.

Sir Robert Phillimore died in 1885, and with him – it might well have seemed – a turbulent and challenging period in the history of English ecclesiastical law also came to a close. By 1895 such controversies as whether 'a clergyman is to be criminally proceeded against for remaining too long on his knees' were described as 'happily dead and buried'.56 Phillimore's successors could again devote their full attention to civil litigation, to the staple business of probate, divorce and admiralty.

Those successors included Sir Robert's only son Walter George Frank Phillimore (1845–1929), who carried on the family tradition in the new legal world. He read Law at Oxford, taking the doctorate of civil law as a Fellow of All Souls (1867–71), and in due course became Chancellor of the Diocese of Lincoln; but instead of joining the virtually defunct Doctors' Commons – which had by then ceased to admit new members – he was called to the Bar by the Middle Temple in 1868, practised in Admiralty and ecclesiastical matters, and received a patent of precedence in 1883.57 Walter served as secretary to his father as Judge of the

---

54 The minister was the father of the person to be commenorated.
55 *Keet v. Smith* (1875) L. R. 4 A. & E. 398 (Court of Arches, on appeal from Sir Robert's son Walter, as Chancellor of Lincoln); (1876) 1 P. D. 73 (Privy Council).
56 Manson, *Some Builders of Our Law*, p. 167.
57 It was the last patent of precedence ever granted: J. Sainty, *A List of English Law Officers, King's Counsel and Holders of Patents of Precedence*, Selden Society, Supplementary Series, 7 (1987), pp. 276, 282. It is not clear why Phillimore was unable or unwilling to accept a patent as Queen's Counsel.

Admiralty, practised in front of him, and also helped him write *Ecclesiastical Law*;[58] it was the son who prepared the second edition of that work in 1895. He was promoted further than his father, becoming a Lord Justice of Appeal in 1913, and Lord Phillimore in 1918 (after his retirement). Sir Robert's great-nephew, Sir Henry Josceline Phillimore (1910–74) also began his judicial career as a judge of the Probate, Divorce and Admiralty Division, in 1959, but he was translated to the Queen's Bench Division in 1962; and in 1968 he too became a Lord Justice of Appeal.

Pedigree of the Lawyer Phillimores

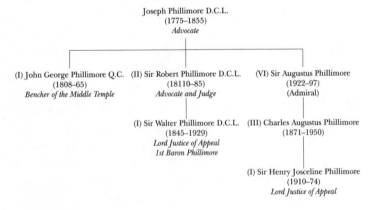

Joseph Phillimore D.C.L.
(1775–1855)
Advocate

(I) John George Phillimore Q.C.
(1808–65)
Bencher of the Middle Temple

(II) Sir Robert Phillimore D.C.L.
(18110–85)
Advocate and Judge

(VI) Sir Augustus Phillimore
(1922–97)
(Admiral)

(I) Sir Walter Phillimore D.C.L.
(1845–1929)
Lord Justice of Appeal
1st Baron Phillimore

(III) Charles Augustus Phillimore
(1871–1950)

(I) Sir Henry Josceline Phillimore
(1910–74)
Lord Justice of Appeal

58 His assistance is recorded in the dedication.

16

The Eclipse of Doctors' Commons

T the time of the sale of Doctors' Commons, in 1865, there were twenty-seven surviving members of the Society of Doctors of Law, some of whom were retired from practice.¹ Five of the surviving practitioners (Addams, Deane, Harding, Phillimore and Twiss) had been given silk in 1858, after the loss of their monopoly of audience; and in the case of Dr Addams this set a precedent for granting that rank to a law graduate who was not a barrister. (The precedent was followed in the case of Dr Tristram in 1881.) The other civilian silks had long before taken the precaution of being called to the common-law Bar,² as had fourteen of the twenty-seven advocates mentioned above, and a few were benchers of their inns. Dr Spinks, being more junior, had been admitted and called to the Bar by the Inner Temple in 1858,³ but did not

---

1 Dr Trenchard had retired as long ago as 1835, and Sir Howard Elphinstone had retired in 1846 on succeeding to his baronetcy. Dr Matcham had resigned his membership in 1835. Unless otherwise stated, biographical details are from *DNB*; *Who Was Who, 1897–1915*; T. S. R. Boase, *Modern English Biography* (1892–1921); and Squibb, *Doctors' Commons*.

2 In addition to those mentioned in the text, Dr Lee (a Bencher of Gray's Inn) took silk in 1864; he died in 1866.

3 He was admitted and called in the same month, by special dispensation.

take silk until 1866. A partial professional assimilation had thus begun, as a prelude to extinction.

The last generation of doctors were a very diverse body of men. While far from being an exclusive caste, three of their number (Jenner-Fust, Phillimore and Robinson) were the sons of advocates, and another (Swabey) a grandson; Dr Robinson was actually born in Doctors' Commons. Some of them, however, were best known for their non-legal activities and achievements. Dr John Lee († 1866), a Fellow of the Royal Society and a founding member of the Royal Astronomical Society, was interested in science, numismatics and archaeology, and possessed a large manuscript collection (mainly derived from Chief Justice Lee and Sir George Lee).4 Sir Travers Twiss († 1897), another Fellow of the Royal Society, was Professor of International Law at King's College London, and then Regius Professor of Civil Law at Oxford. He was an amateur historian, and produced editions of *The Black Book of the Admiralty* and *Bracton* for the Rolls Series. The edition of *Bracton* was badly received by the experts, and Maitland wrote scathing comments into his own copy, now in the Squire Law Library, Cambridge. Undeterred, Twiss completed an edition of *Glanvill* for the Rolls Series, and several copies were printed off after his death; however, on Maitland's advice, the edition was suppressed and most of the copies destroyed.5 Another Professor at King's College London was Sir George Dasent († 1896), who was an Assistant Editor of *The Times*, a Civil Service Commissioner, and a distinguished Norse scholar. Sir John Harding († 1868)

---

4 There is a brief account of his life by H. A. Hanley, *Dr John Lee of Hartwell* (Buckinghamshire Record Office, 1983), with a guide to his papers. See also the article by G. C. Boase in *DNB*, xi, pp. 803–4. The article on Sir George Lee, ibid., xi, pp. 794–95, says that many of his notebooks were still at Hartwell at the end of the nineteenth century; cf. above, p. 123.

5 G. D. G. Hall, ed., *Glanvill* (1965), pp. lxiii–lxiv.

likewise nurtured an interest in philology, and published *An Essay on the Influence of the Welsh Tradition upon European Literature* (1840). Nor were the non-vocational achievements of our doctors confined to literary endeavour. Dr Jenner-Fust († 1904), if we are to credit the entry in *Who Was Who*, was as well known for his contribution to cricket as for his legal expertise;[6] having captained Cambridge in the first inter-university cricket match in 1827, he became President of the M.C.C. in 1833. His Trinity Hall colleague Dr Bayford († 1874) had rowed for Cambridge in the first university boat race.

Several of the group (Addams, 1822–26; Curteis, 1834–44; Robertson, 1844–53;[7] Spinks, 1853–55; Deane and Swabey, 1855–57; Swabey and Tristram, 1858–65) continued the tradition of reporting ecclesiastical cases.[8] Others reported Admiralty cases (Robinson 1838–52, Swabey 1858–59, and Lushington 1860–65). When this civilian tradition was absorbed into the mainstream upon the foundation of the *Law Reports* in 1865, the reporting of ecclesiastical cases continued for a time to be carried on by doctors of law (Tristram, 1869; Middleton, 1869–78; and Pritchard,[9] 1878–86). Very few of the last generation of advocates, however, contributed in any more substantial way to civilian literature. Mention might be made of Twiss's works on international law, especially *The Law of Nations* (1861–63), and of the lesser-known

---

6 He is not to be confused with his more distinguished father, Sir Herbert, who was King's Advocate.

7 Rob. Ecc. Dr Robertson is not to be confused with Dr Robinson, the Admiralty reporter.

8 In addition, Dr Waddilove produced a *Digest of Cases* (1849).

9 Dr Pritchard was not, however, a member of Doctors' Commons. He was the author of *A Digest of the Law and Practice of the Court for Divorce and Matrimonial Causes* (1864; new edn, 1874). This was a revised version of the *Handbook* which he had written in conjunction with W. T. Pritchard, proctor and solicitor, in 1859. It was merely a digest of case law and legislation.

work on matrimonial law by Dr Waddilove,[10] though the palm for novelty must go to Dr Pratt for his *Essay on the Use of Lights by Sea-Going Vessels* (1857), a subject of considerable importance in litigation arising from collisions at sea.[11] Even more recondite, and distinctly unenticing to the general reader – though doubtless of considerable practical utility – was Dr Swabey's *Duties of Parish Officers in Electing Guardians under the Poor-Law Amendment Act* (1835). Books of this type, however useful, were in the category of guides rather than juristic literature.

For a contribution to the literature of ecclesiastical law which deserves a place alongside the famous English canon lawyers of previous generations, only Phillimore stands out.[12] However, Phillimore was not the very last advocate of note, and we should in fairness end our list with a brief notice of Dr Tristram. Thomas Hutchinson Tristram was the last doctor of law admitted to Doctors' Commons – in 1855 – and in the event the last surviving advocate. He pursued a conventional civilian career, becoming Commissary of the Diocese of Canterbury and Chancellor of Hereford, Ripon and London. In the last position, he was obliged to continue the work of Lushington and Phillimore in dealing with the goings on at St Barnabas, Pimlico, and other questions of like nature.[13] On the curtailment of the ecclesiastical jurisdiction, he continued his practice in the new statutory courts and took silk in 1881. He was a reporter under the old order in Doctors' Commons until its dissolution, and later published

---

10 A. Waddilove, *The Laws of Marriage and the Laws of Divorce of England* (1864). He also wrote *Church Patronage Historically, Legally and Morally Considered in Connection with the Offence of Simony* (1854).

11 Dr Pratt also wrote *The Law of Contraband of War* (1856).

12 See the preceding chapter.

13 It is enough to mention *White* v. *Bowron* (1874) L. R. 4 A. & E. 207, in which he held the baldacchino in St Barnabas to be unlawful. For this troublesome church, see above, pp. 139, 140.

a selection of consistory cases from 1872 to 1890. But Dr Tristram's name is familiar to lawyers at the present day solely as a result of his *Treatise on Contentious Probate Practice in the High Court of Justice* (1881), which in 1888 was combined with H. C. Coote's long-established *Practice of the Court of Probate* (1858; ninth edition, 1883) to form 'Tristram and Coote', now in its twenty-eighth edition (1995). Of course, no one today would think of probate as a branch of ecclesiastical law, and indeed the second of these books had been conceived at the moment when it ceased to be so; the authors were consciously making the old learning of Doctors' Commons, in its new statutory context, available to the unspecialised legal profession.

Thomas Hutchinson Tristram D.C.L. (1825–1912), Photograph by Lock and Whitfield, 1882.

From a photograph in the possession of the author

The End

When the Matrimonial, Probate and Admiralty courts were merged into the new High Court of Justice in 1875, as the Probate, Divorce and Admiralty Division, only eleven doctors were still nominally in practice.[14] A quarter of a century later, in 1899, when the last practising serjeant at law died,[15] there remained four doctors (Deane, Fust, Stonestreet and Tristram). The last of the four, as already noted, was Dr Tristram K.C., who died on 8 March 1912. As a practising profession, or at least as a body entitled to practise, they had just managed to outlive the serjeants. However, the Order of Serjeants lingered on in the person of Lord Lindley, the retired Master of the Rolls, until his death in 1921. It could be maintained that Doctors' Commons technically continued in existence even longer, at least until the retirement of Sir Lewis Dibdin K. C. († 1938) as Dean of Arches in 1934,[16] and maybe even beyond.[17] But the scarlet gowns of the doctors and serjeants were to be seen at the Bar no more. They belonged to the rapidly forgotten era before the Royal Courts of Justice were built in the Strand, the twilight

---

14 C. Shaw, *The Inns of Court Calendar* (1877), p. 19, lists thirteen, but includes two (Curteis and Twiss) who had officially retired. When Phillimore became a Justice of the High Court in 1875, he was thereby disqualified from practice.

15 Serjeant Spinks died on 27 December 1899. By a curious coincidence, Dr Thomas Spinks of Doctors' Commons died on 14 January 1899. They were not brothers, and it is not known whether they were otherwise related.

16 Dibdin had not been a practising member of Doctors' Commons, but would have become *ex officio* president (under the terms of the charter of 1768) when he was appointed in 1903, since at that date there were still two other members of the Society alive (Jenner-Fust and Spinks). Upon his retirement, however, there would have been no members at all.

17 See P. Barber, 'The Fall and Rise of Doctors' Commons', *Ecclesiastical Law Journal*, 4 (1996), p. 462.

before the reforms in judicature which had made them in their several ways otiose. It must be a matter of personal opinion and speculation whether the legal world has lost anything of importance with the disappearance of the special expertise of the advocates in Doctors' Commons. If we look only at the last phase of their history, a generous answer to the question may be difficult to afford. But the last survivors were men who for various reasons had entered a doomed profession, whose only hope was to merge with the common-law Bar. Phillimore shone out as an exception. Lord Sumner remarked that 'he belonged to a class of lawyers that has now passed away. He was a scholar both in classical and in modern languages, and a jurist of wide reading ...'[18] If we turn back to the previous generation, we find such qualities more widely spread, but the doctoral intellects were working within an unreformed legal system which could hardly survive much longer. In an age when, as Phillimore put it, every existing institution was required to make out a convincing case against abolition, the extinction seemed inevitable even to most of those at the heart of the system. And yet something of value was perhaps lost in the process, not least the cosmopolitan frame of learning which made Doctors' Commons a centre of European legal culture long before the troubled modern attempts at integration.

18 DNB, xii, p. 1073.

Index